CLASSICS IN EDUCATION
Lawrence A. Cremin, General Editor

☆ ☆ ☆

THE REPUBLIC AND THE SCHOOL
Horace Mann on the Education of Free Men
Edited by Lawrence A. Cremin

AMERICAN IDEAS ABOUT ADULT EDUCATION
1710–1951
Edited by C. Hartley Grattan

DEWEY ON EDUCATION
Introduction and Notes by Martin S. Dworkin

THE SUPREME COURT AND EDUCATION
(Revised and enlarged)
Edited by David Fellman

INTERNATIONAL EDUCATION
A Documentary History
Edited by David G. Scanlon

CRUSADE AGAINST IGNORANCE
Thomas Jefferson on Education
Edited by Gordon C. Lee

CHINESE EDUCATION UNDER COMMUNISM
Edited by Chang-tu Hu

CHARLES W. ELIOT AND POPULAR EDUCATION
Edited by Edward A. Krug

WILLIAM T. HARRIS ON EDUCATION
(in preparation)
Edited by Martin S. Dworkin

THE *EMILE* OF JEAN JACQUES ROUSSEAU
Selections
Translated and Edited by William Boyd

THE MINOR EDUCATIONAL WRITINGS OF
JEAN JACQUES ROUSSEAU
Selected and Translated by William Boyd

PSYCHOLOGY AND THE SCIENCE OF EDUCATION
Selected Writings of Edward L. Thorndike
Edited by Geraldine M. Joncich

THE NEW-ENGLAND PRIMER
Introduction by Paul Leicester Ford

BENJAMIN FRANKLIN ON EDUCATION
Edited by John Hardin Best

THE COLLEGES AND THE PUBLIC
1787–1862
Edited by Theodore Rawson Crane

TRADITIONS OF AFRICAN EDUCATION
Edited by David G. Scanlon

NOAH WEBSTER'S AMERICAN SPELLING BOOK
Introductory Essay by Henry Steele Commager

VITTORINO DA FELTRE
AND OTHER HUMANIST EDUCATORS
By William Harrison Woodward
Foreword by Eugene F. Rice, Jr.

DESIDERIUS ERASMUS
CONCERNING THE AIM AND METHOD
OF EDUCATION
By William Harrison Woodward
Foreword by Craig R. Thompson

JOHN LOCKE ON EDUCATION
Edited by Peter Gay

CATHOLIC EDUCATION IN AMERICA
A Documentary History
Edited by Neil G. McCluskey, S.J.

THE AGE OF THE ACADEMIES
Edited by Theodore R. Sizer

HEALTH, GROWTH, AND HEREDITY
G. Stanley Hall on Natural Education
Edited by Charles E. Strickland and Charles Burgess

TEACHER EDUCATION IN AMERICA
A Documentary History
Edited by Merle L. Borrowman

THE EDUCATED WOMAN IN AMERICA
Selected Writings of Catharine Beecher, Margaret Fuller, and M. Carey Thomas
Edited by Barbara M. Cross

EMERSON ON EDUCATION
Selections
Edited by Howard Mumford Jones

ECONOMIC INFLUENCES UPON EDUCATIONAL PROGRESS IN THE UNITED STATES, 1820–1850
By Frank Tracy Carlton
Foreword by Lawrence A. Cremin

QUINTILIAN ON EDUCATION
Selected and Translated by William M. Smail

ROMAN EDUCATION FROM CICERO TO QUINTILIAN
By Aubrey Gwynn, S.J.

HERBERT SPENCER ON EDUCATION
Edited by Andreas M. Kazamias

JOHN LOCKE'S *OF THE CONDUCT OF THE UNDERSTANDING*
Edited by Francis W. Garforth

STUDIES IN EDUCATION DURING THE AGE OF THE RENAISSANCE, 1400–1600
By William Harrison Woodward
Foreword by Lawrence Stone

JOHN AMOS COMENIUS ON EDUCATION
Introduction by Jean Piaget

HUMANISM AND THE SOCIAL ORDER IN TUDOR ENGLAND
By Fritz Caspari

VIVES' *INTRODUCTION TO WISDOM*
Edited by Marian Leona Tobriner, S.N.J.M.

THE THEORY OF EDUCATION IN THE *REPUBLIC* OF PLATO
By Richard Lewis Nettleship
Foreword by Robert McClintock

UTOPIANISM AND EDUCATION
Robert Owen and the Owenites
Edited by John F. C. Harrison

SCHOOLS OF HELLAS
By Kenneth J. Freeman
Foreword by William M. Calder III

THE EDUCATIONAL THEORIES OF THE SOPHISTS
Edited by James L. Jarrett

SIR THOMAS ELYOT'S
THE BOOK NAMED THE GOVERNOR
Abridged and Edited by John M. Major

JEWISH EDUCATION IN THE UNITED STATES
A Documentary History
Edited by Lloyd P. Gartner

HENRY BARNARD'S *SCHOOL ARCHITECTURE*
Edited by Jean and Robert McClintock

JOHN STUART MILL ON EDUCATION
Edited by Francis W. Garforth

John Stuart Mill on Education

Edited, with an Introduction and Notes, by

FRANCIS W. GARFORTH

TEACHERS COLLEGE PRESS
TEACHERS COLLEGE, COLUMBIA UNIVERSITY
NEW YORK

Library of Congress Catalog
Card Number 75–155230

Manufactured in the United States of America

Foreword

John Stuart Mill held no narrow view of education, believing as he did that it encompassed not only "whatever we do for ourselves and whatever is done for us by others for the express purpose of bringing us somewhat nearer to the perfection of our nature," but also the indirect effects on human character of the laws, the forms of government, the arts of industry, and the modes of social life. Moreover, for all Mill's much-vaunted aversion to public regulation and control, he was well aware that only as government played an active role in requiring and even sponsoring education could a free society on the liberal model be maintained. Yet the proper balance in that effort—between the formal and the informal, the voluntary and the involuntary, the public and the private, the institutional and the individual—was ever a matter of concern to Mill, as he sought to chart a proper course between the perils of tyranny on the one hand and of anarchy on the other.

Mill's ideas were never decisive in the development of nineteenth-century education, though they were widely known in England and contributed significantly to the quality of Victorian intellectual life. In the United States, they were taken up primarily by the genteel reformers of the Gilded Age, but seem to have had little impact on a people already committed to the principle of aggressive state action in the development of universal educational opportunity. That principle has been sharply challenged in recent years by those who in the interest of individual freedom would dismantle large segments of the public education system, or at the very least sharply alter its outlines and character. In the challenge most assuredly lies the making of a spirited debate, to which the relevance of Mill will be undeniable.

LAWRENCE A. CREMIN

Contents

Introduction[1]

By FRANCIS W. GARFORTH

The contribution of James Mill and his son John Stuart to the life of their time was manifold and distinguished. In ardor of idealism and sheer intellectual talent they had few rivals; their influence was correspondingly great and has not yet, one suspects, been fully assessed. James was a Scot, born in 1773 in the village of Northwater Bridge in the county of Forfar. After graduating at the University of Edinburgh he was licensed as a preacher but failed to obtain a parish; he decided therefore in 1802 to seek his fortune in London as a writer and journalist. His energy and ability were such that within three years he was earning enough to pay off his family's debts and provide for a wife. He was married in 1805 and John Stuart, the first child, was born in 1806. Of his mother there is no mention in John's *Autobiography* and little enough elsewhere; she was overshadowed by her husband's brilliance, and the care of a large family gave little opportunity, even if she were capable of it, of ministering to his intellectual needs. On the other hand John's debt to his father is clearly shown—and generously acknowledged—in his description of the extraordinary education he received at his hands; comment on this will be found in a later section.

[1] In the footnotes to this introduction page references are to the present volume unless otherwise stated.

Much of John's education came from the informal influences to which, by design or accident, he was submitted as he grew up. He mentions particularly the stimulus he received from his father's *History of India,* whose proofs he helped to correct at the age of eleven. Important, too, were the summer holidays spent at Jeremy Bentham's country mansion, Ford Abbey, in Somerset, which gave him "the sentiment of a larger and freer existence" and "a sort of poetic cultivation."[2] Another experience of great significance was his year's residence in France with Jeremy's brother, Sir Samuel Bentham; to this he owed the beginning of his lifelong interest in botany. A visit to the Pyrenees gave him his first introduction to lofty mountains, which impressed him deeply "and gave a colour to my tastes through life."[3] In France, too, he "breathed . . . the free and genial atmosphere of Continental life,"[4] which he found in striking contrast with the pettiness of the English society he knew at home; and, of course, he acquired a fluent knowledge of French.[5] It is not surprising that Mill insists repeatedly on the educative force of the general environment; "whatever helps to shape the human being," he tells us in the *Inaugural Address,* is part of his education.[6]

Much of his education he also created for himself, more especially after the years of formal instruction were left behind. Though John never went to a university, he

[2] p. 86.
[3] p. 87.
[4] p. 88.
[5] On this visit to France, see A. J. Mill, *John Mill's Boyhood Visit to France* (Toronto: University of Toronto Press, 1960); also A. Bain, *John Stuart Mill: A Criticism with Personal Recollections* (London: Longmans, Green, 1882) and M. St.J. Packe, *The Life of John Stuart Mill* (London: Secker and Warburg, 1954), pp. 41 ff.
[6] p. 154.

supplied the deficiency by devoting himself to those activities which constitute the most valuable part of an undergraduate's intellectual training—the reading of good books, practice in writing, and discussion with one's peers and with men of learning. Of these last he mentions John Austin, who became the first professor of jurisprudence at University College, London; George Grote, the banker and historian of Greece; David Ricardo, the political economist; and numerous others. In the winter of 1822–23 he founded the Utilitarian Society, which met fortnightly at Bentham's London house to discuss the principles and implications of the philosophy of utility. This lasted for about three years and was followed by a less formal group which met at Grote's house to study important books, of which the first to be chosen was James Mill's *Political Economy*. In 1825 he helped to found the London Debating Society, which attracted to its membership many eminent men of the time and at which John himself was a regular speaker. During these years he was also writing letters and articles for various journals—*The Traveller, The Morning Chronicle, The Westminster Review*—and editing Bentham's manuscript for his *Rationale of Judicial Evidence*. Few students today can hope for a university education as rich in stimulus and learning as this intensely rigorous but largely informal training that Mill imposed upon himself.

In addition to his other activities he was appointed in 1823 to a post as clerk in the East India Company, which at that time was still responsible for a large measure of the civil administration and commercial business of India. His father already held a senior position with the company as assistant to the Examiner of India Correspondence; he was later to become Examiner and, as such, virtually head of the administrative side of its affairs. It was not difficult, therefore, to secure a place for John in the same office. His salary was at first nominal, but the prospects were good and the hours generous enough to allow plenty of leisure for his own pursuits. He stayed with the company until its responsibilities were assumed by the British Government in 1858, by which time he had himself been promoted to Examiner. In the *Autobiography* he acknowledges his debt to the East India Company for the insight his duties gave him into the conduct of public affairs and the necessity for simplicity and clarity of expression.[7]

In 1826 Mill suffered what he calls "a crisis in my mental history"; today we should no doubt refer to it as a nervous breakdown accompanied by depression. That something of the kind should occur is hardly surprising in view of his strenuous and precocious intellectual activity; but there were no doubt deeper causes in the revolt of his nature against the straitjacket of his education. His description of this experience and of his deliverance from it as his feelings were stirred, first by Marmontel's *Mémoires* and then more profoundly by the poetry of Wordsworth, is part of the fascination of the *Autobiography*. The result was a radical change of outlook from orthodox Benthamism as instilled by his father towards a view of human nature which "gave its proper place, among the prime necessities of human well-being, to the internal culture of the individual."[8] All this can be found in the text which follows; there is some further comment later in this introduction.

The period of John's life reviewed thus far is that covered by the portion of the *Autobiography* printed here; it is these early chapters that are most significant

[7] pp. 103–104.
[8] p. 127.

the enfranchisement of women, and national education; he introduced the first proposal for a London County Council (established eventually in 1888); he strove, with only partial success, to bring to justice the Governor of Jamaica for his brutal suppression of an uprising. When he was defeated at the general election of 1868, he returned with relief to his writing and divided his time between London and Avignon, tended by Helen as secretary and housekeeper. It was at Avignon that he died in 1873; he was buried there beside Harriet in the grave he had prepared for them both.

Mill was fortunate in having a professional career which left him ample leisure for writing. Most of his major books have already been mentioned; further reference to his writings will be found in the Bibliographical Note which follows. The best known of them today is perhaps the essay *On Liberty,* which is of course a classic statement of the claims of individuality and personal freedom against authority. *Utilitarianism* and *Three Essays on Religion* are also well known and still have something to contribute to ethical and theological debate. But the most important of his books is the *System of Logic,* begun in 1830 and published in 1843, in which he was the first to bring together deductive and inductive inference into a single body of logic and to attempt a thorough justification of induction as the basis of scientific method. Another important work was the *Principles of Political Economy,* which for long was the standard English treatise on this subject. He was not, it may justly be said, a great scholar, but he had an able, penetrating, and wide-ranging mind. It was also an honest mind, refusing adherence to ideas when he no longer felt able to accept them; in this he was not unlike his godson, the philosopher Bertrand Russell.

PHILOSOPHICAL AND SOCIAL THOUGHT

It is impossible in a few paragraphs to do justice to the complexity of Mill's social thought and its philosophical bases, but some indication can be given of the broad pattern of his ideas and of the sources from which he drew. The utilitarianism commonly associated with his name he took from his father and Jeremy Bentham; what he took, however, he later transformed by additions of his own. Bentham's utilitarianism incorporated three fundamental principles. First, society is a convenient fiction whose only reality lies in "the individual persons who are considered as constituting, as it were, its *members*"; it follows that the interest of the community is "the sum of the interests of the several persons who compose it" and any political or social questions concerning the community can be resolved into questions about individual men and women.[14] Second, the standard by which these interests are to be judged is the principle of utility, "the greatest happiness of all those whose interest is in question."[15] Third, in order to give precision to his notion of happiness he introduced the principle of the "felicific calculus": the happiness of an individual, and so of a society, can be calculated by a simple arithmetical process of adding up pleasures and pains as positive and negative quantities. In all this there is a great deal of confusion which it would be pointless to try to unravel here; but two points are essential for an understanding of Mill. Bentham assumes that society consists of individuals each acting according to self-interest; the purpose of government is to create a situation of minimum conflict between these interests. Further, self-

[14] *Principles of Morals and Legislation*, ch. 1, § 4.
[15] *Ibid.*, ch. 1, § 1, note.

interest, or happiness is purely quantitative; "quantity of pleasure being equal, pushpin is as good as poetry."

Though Mill never abandoned belief in happiness as the principal criterion of ethical choice and the goal of human endeavor, he changed and greatly enriched utilitarianism in two ways. First, he introduced a new conception of the individual, not simply as a unit composing with others the corporate mass of society, but as having value in his own right and as such to be cherished, protected, and developed. This is the central message of the essay *On Liberty:*

> Human nature is not a machine to be built after a model and set to do exactly the work prescribed for it, but a tree which requires to grow and develop itself on all sides, according to the tendency of the inward forces which make it a living thing. . . . In proportion to the development of his individuality each person becomes more valuable to himself, and is therefore capable of being more valuable to others.[16]

He further enriched the concept by his belief that the individual can look beyond self-interest to altruistic ideals which envisage the progressive improvement of society. Second, he introduced into the idea of happiness the criterion of quality: there are different kinds and qualities of happiness, and some of these are preferable to others; poetry *is* better than pushpin, and a preference for the former indicates a higher quality of character in the man who so chooses: "It would be absurd that while, in estimating all other things quality is considered as well as quantity, the estimation of pleasures should be supposed to depend on quantity alone." And even though the higher pleasures elude our grasp, as they are

[16] *On Liberty, Representative Government, The Subjection of Women,* ed. M. G. Fawcett (London: Oxford University Press, 1912), pp. 73, 78.

apt to do, it is something to have reached for them—"better to be Socrates dissatisfied than a fool satisfied."[17] How far Mill's transformation of Benthamism was due to his mental crisis, how far to Harriet Taylor and other friends, how far to the rejection of his father's training, and how far simply to the normal processes of mental growth it is impossible to say; certainly he made of utilitarianism something very different from the doctrine he received from Jeremy Bentham.

Mill was also indebted to the French philosopher Auguste Comte and the followers of his compatriot and onetime associate, the Comte de Saint-Simon. From these came two further formative influences; first, the idea of a "religion of humanity," which substituted for a divine being the ideal of a humanity moving towards its perfection, an ideal which, he wrote in *Three Essays on Religion,* "offers to the imagination and sympathies a large enough object to satisfy any reasonable demand for grandeur of aspiration."[18] The second was the idea that the present time was one of transition from a selfish, aggressive, skeptical period of history (which had lasted since the Reformation) to a new era of justice, co-operation, and enlightenment. Mill was thus enabled to believe in and devote himself to progress and human betterment, a state of society marked by "unchecked liberty of thought, unbounded freedom of individual action in all modes not hurtful to others, but also [by] convictions as to what is right and wrong, useful and pernicious, deeply engraven on the feelings by early education and general unanimity of sentiment."[19]

[17] *Utilitarianism,* ed. M. Warnock (London: Dent, 1962), pp. 258-260; ed. J. B. Schneewind (New York: Collier-Macmillan, 1965), pp. 283-284.

[18] 1874 ed., p. 106; University of Toronto Press, 1969, X, 420.

[19] *Autobiography* (Oxford University Press), pp. 140-141.

From all these various sources there grew a pattern of thought which crystallized thus. Human society is capable of improvement and it is the duty of responsible men and women to promote this. Before society can be improved, however, it must be understood, and a methodology must therefore be established which will give to social studies the firm scientific foundation already enjoyed by the physical sciences; this was a major purpose of the *System of Logic,* in Book VI of which Mill addresses himself to the problem of adapting inductive inference to the peculiar difficulties of the study of society. Social improvement also requires collective action backed by the authority of government. This authority is justified not simply by its practical success in promoting well-being, but also by the extent to which it represents the wishes of its citizens and calls on their participation in government. What is required, then, is a representative democracy expressing the will of the majority through a franchise extended to women and the working class (both were then excluded). However, there are dangers here which must be strenuously avoided, principally the suppression of individuality and the debasing of standards, whether by ignorance or choice, to a commonplace level of mediocrity—what the majority want is not necessarily what is best, and the tyranny it can exercise is no less perilous than that of the autocrat. To avoid these dangers there must be effective safeguards: freedom of thought, speech, and action insofar as they are not harmful to others; education to secure an informed electorate capable of reasoned argument; an elite, both executive and cultural, to supply the expertise and the qualitative standards which the majority lack. In all this there are problems, even inconsistencies, which Mill could not resolve and which are with us still—collective action versus individual initiative, co-operation versus the stimulus of competition, elitism versus egalitarian principles; but we are indebted to him for pointing to some of the essential elements of democracy and its inherent dangers.

EDUCATIONAL THOUGHT

Mill has left us no systematic exposition of his ideas on education. The nearest approach to it is the *Inaugural Address,* but this is directed to university students and is concerned mainly with the content of their studies. Much can be gleaned from comments in the *Autobiography* on his own education, much too from various writings more or less directly concerned with education, for example, the essays *On Genius* and *Civilisation* and the article "Endowments" in Volume IV of *Dissertations and Discussions;* there are also numerous passages in his books and letters which augment these other sources, and from all of them together there emerges a coherent picture of his educational thought. It is this general picture that is our concern in the present section; the *Autobiography* and *Inaugural* receive specific comment later.

At the start of the *Inaugural Address* Mill makes an important distinction between two meanings of education, a wider and a narrower: the former includes every influence that shapes our growth, the latter refers to the specific training given by home and school and one's own attempts at self-improvement. He was keenly conscious of the educational impact of the general environment: "It is a great mistake," he writes, remembering his holidays at Ford Abbey, "to think that children are not benefited by living and growing up among models of beauty";[20] the character of women in Mill's England is

[20] Elliot, *op. cit.,* II, 226.

the result of social conditioning to obedience and subordination; he insists that books and lectures are not the only instruments of education—men are shaped by daily work, by sharing in local government, by the responsibilities of ownership; indeed, school learning is useless "if the circumstances which surround the grown man or woman contradict the lesson."[21] This is not, of course, to deny the need for universal and compulsory formal education:

> There are certain primary elements and means of knowledge which it is in the highest degree desirable that all human beings born into the community should acquire during childhood. . . . It is therefore an allowable exercise of the powers of government to impose on parents the legal obligation of giving elementary instruction to children.[22]

We now demand a far greater minimum of essential education than Mill, but the principle is the same.

Mill's concept of the individual, which was noted in the previous section as a deviation from Benthamism, constitutes an important element in his educational as well as his political thinking. He expounds it principally in Chapter 3 of *On Liberty*, but it is a theme which recurs in much of his writing: the free development of individuality is one of the essentials of well-being; it is both a part and a condition of civilization, instruction, education, culture. It is by the employment of his faculties in choosing and implementing his own plans that a man grows in powers of observation, reasoning, judgment, and the moral qualities of persistence and self-control. Moreover, to the extent that he improves the

[21] "The Claims of Labour," *Dissertations and Discussions* (London, 1859), II, 204.

[22] *Political Economy,* Book V, ch. 11; University of Toronto Press, 1965, III, 948.

quality of his individuality, he increases the value of his contribution to society. From the principle of individuality it follows that knowledge must be firsthand; Mill deplores that cramming of predigested fact which so often passes for instruction—"knowledge comes only from within."[23] There follows too the need for cultivating imagination and sensitivity through poetry and the arts, for individuality is thus uplifted to higher levels of experience. Finally, the principle suggests that a vital source of moral education is what Alfred North Whitehead later called "the vision of greatness"; it is by the inspiration of the ideal embodied in individual character and achievement that others are kindled to pursue a similar perfection for themselves.

Mill's emphasis on individual freedom and spontaneity created a conflict in his thinking between the need for state intervention and the danger of regimentation. This is especially clear in education. He saw plainly enough that education is essential for democracy: only an educated people can be entrusted with the vote—"universal teaching must precede universal enfranchisement."[24] Moreover, education is a principal means to that moral and cultural growth without which the utilitarian ideal of general well-being is unattainable. He also saw that private initiative could not supply the whole of what was needed; the state must play its part. He advocated, therefore, the enforcement by legislation of minimum standards of literacy and numeracy, which it would be the parents' duty to ensure. Where they could not do so, the state must provide the means of in-

[23] *On Genius,* in *Essays on Literature and Society,* ed. J. B. Schneewind (New York: Collier-Macmillan, 1965), p. 92.

[24] *On Liberty, Representative Government, etc.,* p. 278.

struction. The state must share, too, in the provision of informal instruction through libraries, theatres, galleries, and public games—by "every means by which the people can be reached."[25] It must secure the most effective use of educational endowments; it must give financial support to disinterested scholarship and research. But a state *monopoly* of education he strongly deprecates:

It is not endurable that a government should, either *de iure* or *de facto,* have a complete control over the education of the people. . . . A government which can mould the opinions and sentiments of the people from their youth upwards can do with them whatever it pleases.[26]

Regimentation was not the only danger, however, which faced democracy; Mill was appalled at the prospect of a dead level of mediocrity imposed by the masses on a minority which was too weak to resist its pressures: "The natural tendency of representative government, as of modern civilisation, is towards collective mediocrity."[27] One way to combat this, of course, is to allow the greatest possible freedom to the individual, short of injury to others, "for the initiation of all wise or noble things comes and must come from individuals."[28] Another is to encourage the existence of an elite who will raise the general level of intelligence, taste, and culture by their own superior standards:

There is always need of persons not only to discover new truths and point out when what were once truths are true no

[25] "Corporation and Church Property," *Dissertations and Discussions,* I, 28.

[26] *Political Economy,* Book V, ch. 11; University of Toronto Press, 1965, III, 950.

[27] *On Liberty, Representative Government, etc.,* p. 259.

[28] *Ibid.,* p. 82.

longer, but also to commence new practices and set the example of more enlightened conduct and better taste and sense in human life.[29]

From such, he writes to an American correspondent, "civilisation will rain down its influences on the remainder of society."[30]

What has been said thus far suggests a concept of education which fits under the broad heading of "liberal"—a description which, for all its vagueness in common parlance, has definite shape in Mill. The concept is seen most clearly in the *Inaugural Address,* which is a sustained exposition of what he understands by "liberal" in the context of undergraduate studies; but he would not confine it to the university. From his writings as a whole there emerges a picture of liberal education which can be summarized thus: it is an education directed, not to specific vocational goals, but to a broad development of understanding over the widest possible area of knowledge; by cultivating sensitivity, imagination, and mental skills it enriches whatever occupation the student later chooses; it is an education concerned not so much with factual acquisition as with the quality of experience, with truth, not dogma, with discovery in intellectual exploration and the release of individual potential; it requires balance as well as range of studies—humanities as well as science, poetry and the arts as well as logic and mathematics; nor need it exclude manual skills, though Mill has little to say of these save for children of the laboring classes. Among its principal instruments—apart, of course, from books—are discussion (seen at its best, Mill thought, in the Socratic dialogues of Plato), the admiration of greatness, and the infectious influence of

[29] *Ibid.*, p. 79.
[30] Elliot, *op. cit.*, II, 227.

person on person—"real education depends on the contact of human living soul with human living soul."[31] This is a noble educational ideal, more practicable in an age when the impact of technology and specialization had scarcely yet been felt, but helpful and suggestive even for ourselves.

In concluding this section it may be helpful to note the psychological assumptions of Mill's educational thought. These were inherited from his father and belong to the so-called associationist school of psychology. The view that ideas become linked in our minds (apart from being obvious to common sense) was explicitly stated by Aristotle; but the first to use the phrase "association of ideas" was Locke in his *Essay concerning Human Understanding.*[32] Locke states that as a result of custom or habit certain ideas are so connected that when one of them comes to mind the others follow, like the notes of a tune that we know by heart. Locke does not develop this theory, but he notes its importance for the educator, who must guard against the formation in children of harmful or undesirable associations. For Hume it is an essential part of his account of mental processes; association occurs when ideas are regularly linked by resemblance, contiguity, or the relation of cause and effect. In David Hartley's *Observations on Man* (1749) it becomes a full-blown psychological theory: association is a primary mental process and the foundation of all our knowledge. It has the same fundamental importance in James Mill's *Analysis of the Phenomena of the Human Mind* (1829) and in his article on education written in 1818 for the fifth edition of the *Encyclopaedia Britannica.* Later exponents of associationism, though

[31] *Ibid.,* p. 86.
[32] Book II, ch. xxxiii.

not without modification, were Alexander Bain and Herbert Spencer.

It is an empirical theory which derives all mental content from sensory impressions of external objects or introspective awareness of our own feelings. From these, as it were, epistemological atoms the body of our knowledge is assembled. The process is essentially associative; whether by accident or, as in education, by deliberate intent, one idea is linked with another to form sequences, molecular patterns of ideas, which can themselves combine with other sequences to form larger structures. The theory is not only empirical, it is also mechanistic, likening mental processes to the rods and gears of an intricate machine. Some would call it materialistic in a pejorative sense, because it explains, even explains away, the higher functions of the mind by deriving them from simple origins in sensory impressions—a criticism which John Mill himself rebuts in a review of Bain's psychological works.[33] A more fundamental criticism is that it does not do justice to the hormic or purposive element in mental activity: mind, as we experience it in self-consciousness, is *active* in planning and choosing; it envisages desired goals and contrives the means to attain them; this suggests a capacity beyond that of mechanical obedience to patterns of acquired associations. However, for the educator it seemed to offer a simple and almost infallible instrument for the formation of character: given a knowledge of the atomic constituents of experience and of how they are linked into sequences of ideas, it should be possible, by selecting the constituents and controlling the associations, to shape human beings in any desired direction. Among the means of control are

[33] *Dissertations and Discussions,* III, 109 ff.

pleasure and pain, praise and blame, reward and punishment. By skillful use of these the educator can establish associations of attraction and aversion, which, when reinforced by habit to become second nature, constitute well-nigh indelible patterns of behavior. However, they must be established early enough and firmly enough, as Mill saw when surveying his own education, to withstand the destructive power of analysis in adolescence and early manhood.[34] As a single, all-explanatory psychological principle, association succumbed to the results of research, which revealed its inadequacy to explain the full range of mental phenomena; but this is not to deny that it plays some part in mental processes, and one which is sufficiently important to warrant the attention of the educator.

THE AUTOBIOGRAPHY

The first draft of Mill's *Autobiography* was written between 1854 and 1856. It was afterwards revised, and then brought up to date in the winter of 1869-70.[35] It was edited by his stepdaughter, Helen Taylor, and published posthumously in 1873. Like so many of his later publications, it was intended, if not strictly as a joint work with Harriet, at least as a manifesto of their intellectual and spiritual life together. Because of her death in 1858 these hopes were only partially fulfilled. The first draft was not essentially different (except in length) from the final version. Mill himself had already deleted from an early version some harsh reflections on his mother's character,[36] and Helen omitted passages

[34] pp. 122-123.
[35] Packe, *op. cit.*, pp. 368-370, 477.
[36] *Ibid.*, p. 33: "That rarity in England, a really warmhearted

amounting to a few pages which she thought it improper at that time to include—mostly concerned with his relations with James Mill and Harriet.

The *Autobiography,* of which rather less than half is printed here, is a strangely moving human document, remarkable almost as much for what it omits as for its account of Mill's intellectual development and his involvement in the social and political endeavors of his time. He tells us nothing of his mother or of any other member of the family save the father to whom he owed so much; and little enough of his life's great passion, his love for Harriet Taylor. Of the mystical and sensitive side of his nature, clearly revealed in his other writings, we have only rare glimpses here. Essentially the book is a record of Mill's intellectual growth and achievement, and of his contribution to the progress of reform in the early and middle years of the nineteenth century. Incidentally it is also a record of that progress itself, at least so far as Mill was involved in it. Finally, and for our present purpose most significantly, it is a record of an extraordinary educational experiment, carefully described and submitted to the mature criticism of a singularly acute mind.

The educational interest of the early chapters is threefold: there is the education itself, beginning at the

---

mother, would in the first place have made my father a totally different being, and in the second would have made the children grow up loving and being loved. But my mother with the very best intentions only knew how to pass her life in drudging for them. Whatever she could do for them she did, and they liked her because she was kind to them; but to make herself loved, looked up to, or even obeyed, required qualities which she unfortunately did not possess. I thus grew up in the absence of love and in the presence of fear; and many and indelible are the effects of this bringing up in the stunting of my moral growth."

precocious age of three and guided by firmly held psychological principles to deliberate goals; there is the question of its success or failure; and there is John's assessment of it. James Mill's theory of education, expounded in his article in the supplement to the fifth edition of the *Encyclopaedia Britannica,* referred to above, was indebted to Helvetius and Hartley for its psychological bases and to Bentham for its overriding purpose.[37] It assumed that the mind, virtually a blank at birth, could be shaped in any desired direction by careful exposure to the right experiences; as a result of mental association, such experiences, regularly repeated in appropriate sequence, created tendencies to specific kinds of behavior. Given, then, a sufficient knowledge of mental processes and sufficient control of environment, the educator can make of a child almost all that he wishes him to be—not quite all, since individual differences remain, but enough at least to grant that "all the difference which exists between classes or bodies of men is the effect of education." And if classes of men, why not the whole human race?—"What a field for exertion! What a prize to be won!"[38] As for the purpose of it—"The end of education is to render the individual as much as possible an instrument of happiness."[39] To such a theory and such a purpose the young John Stuart was submitted; he was to be trained, by methods derived from an associative psychology of supposedly indubitable validity, to further the utilitarian doctrine of happiness and human betterment.

How far was the attempt successful? To the extent at least that John succeeded his father as leader of the util-

[37] On these see p. 46 note, and pp. 144, 145.

[38] W. H. Burston, ed., *James Mill on Education* (London: Cambridge University Press, 1969), p. 52.

[39] *Ibid.,* p. 41.

itarians, that he devoted himself untiringly to the promotion of social reform, that he became a rigorous and honest thinker, and that he wrote with authority on logic, political economy, and other subjects. On the other side of the balance one must place John's radical departure from orthodox utilitarianism by introducing estimations of quality as well as quantity into the assessment of happiness. More significant, however, is the nervous breakdown he suffered at the age of twenty. Though due in part, no doubt, to the sheer stress of overwork, its fundamental cause was surely the rebellion of his fundamental nature against the suppression of its emotional and aesthetic bent. Of this Mill himself was aware (though not in Freudian terms) when he wrote the *Autobiography:* for two or three years of his life, he admits, the description of a Benthamite "as a mere reasoning machine"[40] was not altogether untrue of himself; he notes the absence in his education of "poetic culture" and a "superabundance of the discipline antagonistic to it, that of mere logic and analysis."[41] The result, he tells us in Chapter 5, was that he was "left stranded at the commencement of my voyage with a well equipped ship and a rudder but no sail, without any real desire for the ends which I had been so carefully fitted out to work for"[42]—a machine without motive power. The crisis itself and Mill's later development were a triumph of nature over nurture, the vindication of an individuality quelled by its upbringing.

It is not only the general tenor and purpose of his education that Mill finds fault with but also its practical details. He condemns the monitorial method whereby he was made to teach the younger children what he had

[40] p. 109. [41] p. 110. [42] p. 123.

himself only recently learned. He notes that his father's teaching was deficient in practical illustration—he trusted "too much to the intelligibleness of the abstract when not embodied in the concrete."[43] He lacked the companionship of his peers. He received no training in manual skills and "always remained inexpert in anything requiring manual dexterity."[44] In short, it was an education "more fitted for training me to *know* than to *do*."[45] On the other hand there was much in his education that John could commend, and it would be unjust to his father to ignore this. He mentions in particular his training in logic and the detection of fallacy. Of especial value too was his father's practice of encouraging the habit of inquiry—"Anything that could be found out by thinking I never was told until I had exhausted my efforts to find it out for myself."[46] Moreover his mind was never merely crammed by simple memorization —"he strove to make the understanding not only go along with every step of the teaching, but, if possible, precede it."[47] Evidently James Mill was a teacher of no ordinary merit; and for all its genuine deficiencies, arising from excess of zeal and inadequate psychology, his education gave John "an advantage of a quarter of a century over my contemporaries."[48]

THE INAUGURAL ADDRESS

When universities were first founded on the continent of Europe, a system of internal government was established under a rector who was endowed with civil and criminal jurisdiction over members of the university; he might

[43] p. 60. [45] p. 70. [47] p. 66.
[44] p. 70. [46] p. 66. [48] p. 65.

be elected by the students, by the teaching body, or by both. St. Andrews, the earliest of the Scottish universities, was founded in 1411; here the third method of suffrage was adopted, and its rector was originally elected by students, teachers, and resident graduates. However, the students lost their right of suffrage in 1475, and it was not fully restored until 1824. In its present form the rectorship dates from the Universities Act of 1858, by which the rector was made the President of the University Court and entitled to preside over the General Council in the absence of the chancellor. He is elected by matriculated students of the university for a period of three years. There have been many distinguished rectors since Mill's time, including James Barrie, Rudyard Kipling, Fridtjof Nansen, and Lord Snow; the present holder of the office (1967–1970) is Lord Constantine. The duties of the rector are now mainly ornamental; he is expected to visit the university and to address the students.[49]

Mill was elected to the office in 1865 without his permission. He had shortly before agreed to nomination as candidate for Westminster at the forthcoming parliamentary election, and was much involved in political matters. He therefore wished to decline the honor but agreed to accept it on the understanding that the rectorial address might be postponed; it was eventually delivered on February 1, 1867. The report in *The Times,* Saturday, February 2, states:

> About 190 students were present, the Arts students being in academic costume. The Vice-Chancellor opened the proceed-

[49] For further details of the office of rector, see A. Morgan, *Scottish University Studies* (London: Oxford University Press, 1933), ch. 2.

ings with prayer in Latin, and afterwards administered the University oath. The Rector was then invested with the robe of office, after which the Vice-Chancellor presented him with the degree of Doctor of Laws.

Mr. Mill then delivered his address on the subject of a university education, which was listened to with sustained attention and cordially applauded. It occupied about two hours in delivery.

Bain's life of Mill gives the duration as three hours,[50] but in either case the speech was inordinately and surely unnecessarily protracted. On the reception given to it, Bain mentions "the vociferous applause of the Divinity students at the free-thought passage."[51]

At the start of the address Mill makes a valuable distinction between a broader and a narrower meaning of "education": the former signifies "whatever helps to shape the human being, to make the individual what he is or hinder him from being what he is not"; the latter, "the culture which each generation purposely gives to those who are to be its successors."[52] The one refers to the total (and often fortuitous) impact of environment, the other to the deliberate initiation of youth into the life of a society. Mill confines himself to the second of these and proceeds to describe the education which he deems appropriate to a university; in so doing he commits himself firmly to the ideal of a liberal education, which he expounds both in general terms and by noting the contributions made to it from particular areas of study. He thus furthers the debate which attracted contributions from some of the best minds of nineteenth-century England, including his younger contemporary, Matthew

[50] Bain, *op. cit.*, p. 126.
[51] *Ibid.*, p. 128, see pp. 215 ff. of *Inaugural Address*.
[52] p. 154.

Arnold.[53] The function of a university, he explains, is not to impart professional knowledge or professional skills but to provide "capable and cultivated human beings" who will "bring the light of general culture to illuminate the technicalities of a special pursuit."[54] It is to train students to perceive the principles which underlie knowledge and thus "to methodise" it, to acquire "a comprehensive and connected view," and to understand "the modes in which the human intellect proceeds from the known to the unknown."[55]

There are three main areas of culture which contribute to this purpose—the intellectual, the moral, and the aesthetic. In the first of these Mill includes classics, the sciences, mathematics, logic, political and historical studies, and law—a vast and daunting program matched rather to the capacity of a J. S. Mill (who never attended a university) than to the ordinary student. *Direct* moral education is the responsibility, not of the school or university, but of the home and social environment; the moral influence of a university consists "in the pervading tone of the place," in the contagious example of teachers, in the presenting of all knowledge "as chiefly a means to worthiness of life."[56] A university must offer its students "the accumulated treasure of the thoughts of mankind," an indispensable part of which consists of what "the best

[53] Among nineteenth-century books which consider this theme are: Herbert Spencer's *Education* (1861); John Henry Newman's *The Idea of a University* (publ. 1873, but the initial lectures were given in 1852); Thomas H. Huxley's *A Liberal Education and Where to Find It* (1868) and other essays in Vol. III of *Collected Essays;* and *Essays on a Liberal Education* (1867), ed. by F. W. Farrar. On Matthew Arnold see the recent edition of his educational writings by P. Smith and G. Summerfield, *Matthew Arnold and the Education of the New Order* (London: Cambridge University Press, 1969).

[54] pp. 155–156. [55] pp. 156–157. [56] p. 212.

and wisest individual men have thought on the great subjects of morals and religion."[57] Finally, in his discussion of aesthetic culture Mill makes a noble and at times impassioned plea for the cultivation of lofty feelings, of the sense of the sublime, of mystery, beauty, and the ideal of perfection. "The more prosaic our ordinary duties, the more necessary it is to keep up the tone of our minds by frequent visits to that higher region of thought and feeling in which every work seems dignified in proportion to the ends for which and the spirit in which it is done."[58]

There is much that is good in the address and much with which one must disagree. On the one hand, Mill pleads for a balanced education which draws on all major areas of human experience. He insists on the value of language learning for clarification of thought and meaning and for insight into political and cultural life—coupling this with a salutary warning against wasting time on superfluities like verse (or even prose) composition. Equally he insists on the contribution of mathematics and science to the pursuit of truth by training in accuracy of thought and interpretation of evidence. One cannot help but be impressed by his claim that "it is a very imperfect education which trains the intelligence only but not the will,"[59] and admire the lofty sentiments of his closing paragraphs. As for his rejection of "dogmatic inculcation from authority of what the teacher deems true" and his assertion that "a university ought to be a place of free speculation,"[60] these surely deserve the applause not only of Mill's contemporaries but also of our own university malcontents.

On the other hand, Mill clearly relies too heavily on

[57] p. 212.
[58] p. 225.
[59] p. 211.
[60] pp. 214, 216.

the doctrine of formal training—an offshoot of his association psychology: no doubt the study of classics or of science leaves some residue of skill and attitude in addition to remembered fact, but the amount of such residue that can be generalized and transferred to other areas of study is now known to be less than Mill supposed. This does not wholly invalidate, but it certainly weakens, his claim for the value of specific subjects in contributing to the general education of students—that, for instance, "scientific education teaches us to think, and literary education to express our thoughts."[61] Again, it is difficult now, in a world very different from Mill's, to accept his view that "universities are not intended to teach the knowledge required to fit men for some special mode of gaining their livelihood";[62] a narrow professionalism is as deplorable as a superficial dilettantism, but life is too short and economic needs too pressing for the total exclusion of what a student may require for his profession. Finally—though this is not all that can be said—Mill's program of studies owes as much to the memory of his own education as to any deliberate concern with the educational needs of the 1860's. The address displays repeatedly the pattern, emphases, and methods of his own studies. Thus he exaggerates the importance of classics; modern languages he will not have *taught* because "they are so much more easily acquired by intercourse with those who use them in daily life." History and geography need no place in the curriculum ("except in elementary schools for children of the labouring classes whose subsequent access to books is limited"), for no one ever really learned them except by private reading.[63] He tends, too, to assess the capacity of students by his

[61] p. 160. [62] p. 155. [63] pp. 167, 168.

own, and this leads him to vastly overload the university curriculum and to attack the "strangely limited estimate of what it is possible for human beings to learn."[64]

For all this, the address is a notable contribution to the contemporary debate on liberal education and is not without its message for today. A century prolific in change of every kind has given new shape and content to many of our educational concepts and has altered significantly our expectation of a university education. But the needs of human beings are much the same now as in Mill's time. "Men are men," he rightly reminds us, "before they are lawyers or physicians or merchants or manufacturers"[65]—or anything else. In a world obsessed with material productivity this is a truth we neglect at our peril.

BIBLIOGRAPHICAL NOTE

Mill's first major publication was his edition in five volumes of Bentham's *Rationale of Judicial Evidence,* prepared from the manuscript and published with an editor's preface in 1827. The first extensive work of his own was *A System of Logic,* begun in 1830 and published in 1843; at that time the book marked a notable advance in the formulation of scientific method, and it still has interest for the modern reader, especially in its attempt to devise a proper method for the study of society. *Essays on Some Unsettled Questions of Political Economy* followed in 1844 (though it was written more than ten years earlier), but this was only the precursor to his larger work, *Principles of Political Economy,* pub-

[64] p. 164. [65] p. 156.

lished in two volumes in 1848 and described as "a joint production with my wife"; this too was an important book in its day. The essay *On Liberty*—also, in conception at least, a joint work with Harriet—appeared in 1859, and thenceforth came a number of books, all of which had been planned and discussed with her; these included *Thoughts on Parliamentary Reform* (1859), *Considerations on Representative Government* (1861), *Utilitarianism* (published in *Fraser's Magazine* in 1861 and separately in 1863), and *The Subjection of Women* (written in 1861, published in 1869). Another major work, *An Examination of Sir William Hamilton's Philosophy,* came out in 1865; Sir William was professor of logic and metaphysics at Edinburgh, and in this protracted critique Mill indirectly gives a statement of his own metaphysical position.

Meanwhile Mill had brought together a number of occasional writings and published them in two volumes of *Dissertations and Discussions* in 1859; a third volume appeared in 1867 and a fourth in 1875. *Auguste Comte and Positivism* was published in 1865, reprinted from *The Westminster Review.* In 1869 came an edition of James Mill's *Analysis of the Phenomena of the Human Mind;* for this John wrote a preface and added a number of notes, some written by himself and others by Alexander Bain, Andrew Findlater, and George Grote. The *Autobiography* and *Three Essays on Religion,* both edited by Helen Taylor, were published posthumously in 1873 and 1874 respectively.

In addition to the above works, Mill was a lifelong contributor to journals and periodicals. Almost all his published writings, including reviews and letters to the press, are listed in a record kept by Mill himself (or at least under his direction, for only the first page is in his writing); this has been edited by N. MacMinn, J. R. Hainds, and J. M. McCrimmon and published in 1945 as *Bibliography of the Published Writings of John Stuart Mill* (Evanston, Ill.: Northwestern University Press). The serious student of Mill will find this bibliography indispensable.

Various selections of Mill's writings have been published from time to time. *Four Dialogues of Plato,* edited by Ruth Borchardt (London: Watts, 1946), brings together notes and translations first published in *The Monthly Repository,* 1834–1835. *Mill on Bentham and Coleridge,* edited with an introduction by F. R. Leavis (London: Chatto and Windus, 1950), reproduces Mill's essays on two men who deeply influenced him and the age in which he lived. Wider, but still specialized, selections are available in *Mill's Essays on Literature and Society* and *Mill's Ethical Writings,* both edited by J. B. Schneewind and published by Collier-Macmillan, New York, 1965. A selection of his ethical writings has also been edited by Mary Warnock (London: Collins, 1962); entitled *Utilitarianism,* it includes not only this work but also *On Liberty,* the essay on Bentham, and extracts from Bentham and John Austin. *Selected Writings of John Stuart Mill,* edited by Maurice Cowling (New York: New American Library, 1968) aims at presenting Mill's defense of liberty within the wider context of his thought on man, society, and religion. Two further selections may be mentioned, that of Dent's Everyman's Library (London, 1910) with an introduction by A. D. Lindsay and including *Utilitarianism, On Liberty,* and *Representative Government,* and Gertrude Himmelfarb's *Essays on Politics and Culture* (New York: Doubleday, 1962).

The *Autobiography* is available in editions by H. J.

Laski (London: Oxford University Press, 1924) and by Asa Briggs (New York: New American Library, 1964). Both have the incomplete text as edited by Helen Taylor (1873); the full text can be found in the Columbia University edition of 1924 (see below, p. 40). Of interest for comparison is J. Stillinger's *The Early Draft of J. S. Mill's Autobiography* (Urbana, Ill.: University of Illinois Press, 1961). Until recently the only collection of Mill's letters was that of H. S. R. Elliot, *The Letters of John Stuart Mill* (London: Longmans, Green, 1910); for the first part of Mill's life this has now been superseded by F. E. Mineka's *Earlier Letters of John Stuart Mill, 1812–1848* (2 vols.; Toronto: University of Toronto Press, 1963). The *Inaugural Address* is included in the first of Schneewind's selections already noted; it also appears in F. A. Cavenagh's *James and John Stuart Mill on Education* (London: Cambridge University Press, 1931, now long out of print), which is valuable for its inclusion of James Mill's article on education.

A complete edition of Mill's writings, in about thirteen volumes, is now in preparation by the University of Toronto Press (which also publishes a Mill newsletter); already published are Mineka's edition of his early letters, vols. XII and XIII, and *Principles of Political Economy* (1965), vols. II and III, *Essays on Economics and Society* (1967), vols. IV and V, and *Essays on Ethics, Religion and Society* (1969), vol. X, these last three edited by J. M. Robson.

It is impossible within the compass of this note to offer anything approaching a full bibliography of works on J. S. Mill; below under two headings are listed books and a few articles which the student will find valuable for one aspect or another of Mill's life and work; many of the books have extensive bibliographies.

BIOGRAPHICAL

Bain, A. *John Stuart Mill: A Criticism with Personal Recollections* (London: Longmans, Green, 1882; New York: Augustus M. Kelley, 1969); this is an interesting account of Mill by a friend who knew him well.

———. *James Mill* (London: Longmans, Green, 1882).

Borchardt, R. *John Stuart Mill: The Man* (London: Watts, 1957).

Courtney, W. L. *The Life of John Stuart Mill* (London: Scott, 1889).

Hayek, F. A. *John Stuart Mill and Harriet Taylor* (London: Routledge and Kegan Paul, 1951).

Letwin, S. R. *The Pursuit of Certainty: David Hume, Jeremy Bentham, John Stuart Mill, Beatrice Webb* (London: Cambridge University Press, 1965).

Levi, A. W. "The Mental Crisis of John Stuart Mill," *Psychoanalytic Review*, XXXII (January 1945).

Mill, A. J. *John Mill's Boyhood Visit to France* (Toronto: University of Toronto Press, 1960); an edition of the diary which Mill kept during this visit.

———. "John Stuart Mill's Visit to Wordsworth, 1831," *The Modern Language Review*, XLIV, 3 (July 1949).

Packe, M. St.J. *The Life of John Stuart Mill* (London: Secker and Warburg, 1954); this is the standard life at present.

Pappé, H. O. *John Stuart Mill and the Harriet Taylor Myth* (London: Cambridge University Press; Melbourne: Melbourne University Press, 1960).

Robson, J. M. "Artist and Scientist: Harriet Taylor and John Stuart Mill," *Queen's Quarterly* (Kingston, Ontario, Canada), No. 73 (1966).

GENERAL

Alexander, E. *Matthew Arnold and John Stuart Mill* (London: Routledge and Kegan Paul, 1965).

Anschutz, R. P. *The Philosophy of J. S. Mill* (London: Oxford University Press, 1953).

Berlin, I. *John Stuart Mill and the Ends of Life* (London: Council of Christians and Jews, 1959).

Britton, K. *John Stuart Mill* (Harmondsworth: Penguin Books, 1953).

Burston, W. H., ed. *James Mill on Education* (London: Cambridge University Press, 1969); this includes the article *Education* and another, *Schools for All;* it makes interesting background reading for John's *Autobiography.*

Cowling, M. *Mill and Liberalism* (London: Cambridge University Press, 1963).

Davidson, W. L. *Political Thought in England: The Utilitarians from Bentham to J. S. Mill* (London: Home University Library, 1915; Oxford University Press, 1947).

Halévy, E. *The Growth of Philosophic Radicalism,* trans. M. Morris (London: Faber and Faber, 1934).

Hamburger, J. *Intellectuals in Politics: John Stuart Mill and the Philosophical Radicals* (New Haven, Conn.: Yale University Press, 1965).

Mueller, I. W. *John Stuart Mill and French Thought* (Urbana, Ill.: University of Illinois Press, 1956).

Plamenatz, J. P. *The English Utilitarians,* 2nd ed. (Oxford: Blackwell, 1958).

Price, A. "J. S. Mill and the Combination of Logic and Poetry in Education," *Researches and Studies,* No. 34 (October 1962).

Radcliff, P., ed. *Limits of Liberty: Studies of Mill's* On Liberty (Belmont, Calif.: Wadsworth, 1966).

Rees, J. C. *Mill and His Early Critics* (Leicester: University College, 1956).

Robson, J. M. *The Improvement of Mankind: The Social and Political Thought of J. S. Mill* (Toronto: University of Toronto Press; London: Routledge and Kegan Paul, 1968).

Schneewind, J. B. *Mill: A Collection of Critical Essays* (London: Macmillan, 1969); a valuable collection of articles concerned with the philosophical aspects of Mill's thought.

Stephen, L. *The English Utilitarians* (3 vols.; London: Duckworth, 1900); the third volume is a valuable study of J. S. Mill's life and work.

West, E. G. "Liberty and Education: J. S. Mill's Dilemma," *Philosophy*, April 1965.

Woods, T. *Poetry and Philosophy: A Study in the Thought of J. S. Mill* (London: Hutchinson, 1961).

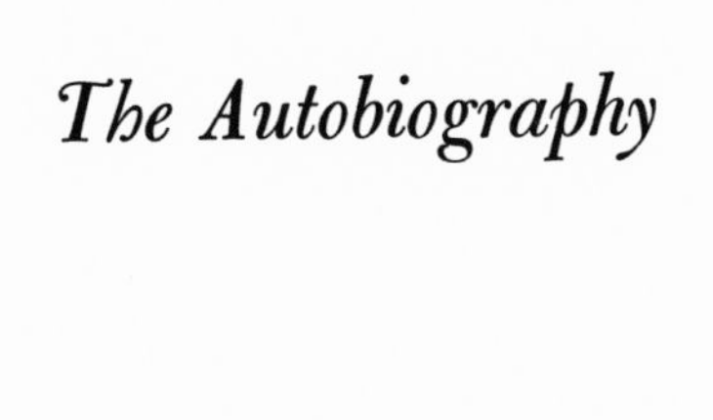
The Autobiography

A NOTE ON THE TEXT

The text which follows is taken, with some minor alterations to punctuation and typography, from the first edition of 1873. This was edited by Mill's step-daughter, Helen Taylor, who deleted from the manuscript a number of passages (about a half-dozen pages in all) which she felt should not be made public at that time. The full text is printed in the John Jacob Coss edition of Columbia University Press, New York (ed. R. Howson, 1924, reprinted 1944, 1948).

Only those parts of the *Autobiography* are printed here which relate to Mill's education and upbringing up to the time of his mental crisis in 1826 and 1827.

I

Childhood and Early Education

It seems proper that I should prefix to the following biographical sketch some mention of the reasons which have made me think it desirable that I should leave behind me such a memorial of so uneventful a life as mine. I do not for a moment imagine that any part of what I have to relate can be interesting to the public as a narrative or as being connected with myself. But I have thought that in an age in which education and its improvement are the subject of more, if not of profounder, study than at any former period of English history, it may be useful that there should be some record of an education which was unusual and remarkable, and which, whatever else it may have done, has proved how much more than is commonly supposed may be taught, and well taught, in those early years which, in the common modes of what is called instruction, are little better than wasted. It has also seemed to me that in an age of transition in opinions there may be somewhat both of interest and of benefit in noting the successive phases of any mind which was always pressing forward, equally ready to learn and to unlearn either from its own thoughts or from those of others. But a motive which weighs more with me than either of these is a desire to make acknowledgement of the debts which my intellectual and moral development owes to other persons, some of them of recognised eminence, others less known than they deserve to be, and the one to whom most of all is due, one whom the world had no opportunity of knowing.[1] The reader whom these things do not interest has only himself to blame if he reads farther, and I do not desire any other indulgence from him than that of bearing in mind that for him these pages were not written.

I was born in London on the 20th of May, 1806, and was the eldest son of James Mill, the author of the *History of British India.* My father, the son of a petty tradesman and (I believe) small farmer at Northwater Bridge, in the county of Angus, was, when a boy, recommended by his abilities to the notice of Sir John Stuart of Fettercain, one of the Barons of the Exchequer in Scotland, and was, in consequence, sent to the University of Edinburgh at the expense of a fund established by Lady Jane Stuart (the wife of Sir John Stuart) and some other ladies for educating young men for the Scottish Church. He there went through the usual course of study and was licensed as a preacher, but never followed the profession, having satisfied himself that he could not believe the doctrines of that or any other Church. For a few years he was a private tutor in various families in Scotland, among others that of the Marquis of Tweeddale, but ended by taking up his residence in London and devoting himself to authorship. Nor had he any other means of support until 1819, when he obtained an appointment in the India House.

In this period of my father's life there are two things which it is impossible not to be struck with, one of them unfortunately a very common circumstance, the other a

[1] His wife, Harriet.—F. W. G.

most uncommon one. The first is that in his position, with no resource but the precarious one of writing in periodicals, he married and had a large family—conduct than which nothing could be more opposed, both as a matter of good sense and of duty, to the opinions which, at least at a later period of life, he strenuously upheld. The other circumstance is the extraordinary energy which was required to lead the life he led, with the disadvantages under which he laboured from the first and with those which he brought upon himself by his marriage. It would have been no small thing had he done no more than to support himself and his family during so many years by writing without ever being in debt or in any pecuniary difficulty, holding, as he did, opinions both in politics and in religion which were more odious to all persons of influence and to the common run of prosperous Englishmen in that generation than either before or since; and being not only a man whom nothing would have induced to write against his convictions, but one who invariably threw into everything he wrote as much of his convictions as he thought the circumstances would in any way permit; being, it must also be said, one who never did anything negligently, never undertook any task, literary or other, on which he did not conscientiously bestow all the labour necessary for performing it adequately. But he, with these burdens on him, planned, commenced and completed the *History of India,* and this in the course of about ten years—a shorter time than has been occupied (even by writers who had no other employment) in the production of almost any other historical work of equal bulk and of anything approaching to the same amount of reading and research. And to this is to be added that during the whole period a considerable part of almost every day was employed in the instruction of his children, in the case of one of whom, myself, he exerted an amount of labour, care and perseverance rarely, if ever, employed for a similar purpose in endeavouring to give, according to his own conception, the highest order of intellectual education.

A man who in his own practice so vigorously acted up to the principle of losing no time was likely to adhere to the same rule in the instruction of his pupil. I have no remembrance of the time when I began to learn Greek; I have been told that it was when I was three years old. My earliest recollection on the subject is that of committing to memory what my father termed vocables, being lists of common Greek words with their signification in English, which he wrote out for me on cards.[2] Of grammar until some years later I learnt no more than the inflexions of the nouns and verbs, but after a course of vocables proceeded at once to translation; and I faintly remember going through Aesop's *Fables,* the first Greek book which I read. The *Anabasis,* which I remember better, was the second. I learnt no Latin until my eighth year. At that time I had read under my father's tuition a number of Greek prose authors, among whom I remember the whole of Herodotus and of Xenophon's *Cyropaedia* and *Memorials of Socrates,* some of the lives of the philosophers by Diogenes Laertius, part of Lucian, and Isocrates *ad Demonicum* and *ad Nicoclem.* I also read in 1813 the first six dialogues (in the common arrangement) of Plato, from the *Euthyphron* to the *Theaetetus* inclusive, which last dialogue, I venture to think, would have been better omitted, as it was totally impossible I should understand it. But my father in all his teaching demanded of me not only the utmost that I

[2] "Vocables" are the words themselves, not the lists.—F. W. G.

could do, but much that I could by no possibility have done. What he was himself willing to undergo for the sake of my instruction may be judged from the fact that I went through the whole process of preparing my Greek lessons in the same room and at the same table at which he was writing; and as in those days Greek and English lexicons were not, and I could make no more use of a Greek and Latin lexicon than could be made without having yet begun to learn Latin, I was forced to have recourse to him for the meaning of every word which I did not know. This incessant interruption he, one of the most impatient of men, submitted to and wrote under that interruption several volumes of his *History* and all else that he had to write during those years.

The only thing besides Greek that I learnt as a lesson in this part of my childhood was arithmetic; this also my father taught me; it was the task of the evenings and I well remember its disagreeableness. But the lessons were only a part of the daily instruction I received. Much of it consisted in the books I read by myself and my father's discourses to me, chiefly during our walks. From 1810 to the end of 1813 we were living in Newington Green, then an almost rustic neighbourhood. My father's health required considerable and constant exercise, and he walked habitually before breakfast, generally in the green lanes towards Hornsey. In these walks I always accompanied him, and with my earliest recollections of green fields and wild flowers is mingled that of the account I gave him daily of what I had read the day before. To the best of my remembrance this was a voluntary rather than a prescribed exercise. I made notes on slips of paper while reading and from these in the morning walks I told the story to him; for the books were chiefly histories, of which I read in this manner a great number: Robertson's histories, Hume, Gibbon; but my greatest delight, then and for long afterwards, was Watson's *Philip the Second and Third.* The heroic defence of the Knights of Malta against the Turks, and of the revolted provinces of the Netherlands against Spain excited in me an intense and lasting interest. Next to Watson my favourite historical reading was Hooke's *History of Rome.* Of Greece I had seen at that time no regular history except school abridgements and the last two or three volumes of a translation of Rollin's *Ancient History,* beginning with Philip of Macedon. But I read with great delight Langhorne's translation of Plutarch. In English history, beyond the time at which Hume leaves off, I remember reading Burnet's *History of his Own Time,* though I cared little for anything in it except the wars and battles, and the historical part of the *Annual Register* from the beginning to about 1788, where the volumes my father borrowed for me from Mr. Bentham[3] left off. I felt a lively interest in Frederick of Prussia during his difficulties and in Paoli, the Corsican patriot; but when I came to the American War, I took my part, like a child as I was (until set right by my father) on the wrong side, because it was called the English side. In these frequent talks about the books I read he used, as

[3] Jeremy Bentham (1748–1832) was a great friend of the Mill family and a major influence on John Stuart; see below, pp. 85–86; and for his influence on J. S. Mill, pp. 94–97. His central interest was the reform of law and of judicial and social institutions; his achievements in these fields, rather than the ethical utilitarianism which formed the somewhat slender philosophical basis of his ideas, constitute his claim to fame. Among his principal written works are *An Introduction to the Principles of Morals and Legislation* (1789) and *Rationale of Judicial Evidence* (5 vols., 1827), the latter of which was edited for him by J. S. Mill; but he also wrote on economics, prisons, and parliamentary reform. See also pp. 10–12.—F. W. G.

opportunity offered, to give me explanations and ideas respecting civilisation, government, morality, mental cultivation, which he required me afterwards to restate to him in my own words. He also made me read, and give him a verbal account of, many books which would not have interested me sufficiently to induce me to read them of myself: among others, Millar's *Historical View of the English Government,* a book of great merit for its time and which he highly valued; Mosheim's *Ecclesiastical History,* McCrie's *Life of John Knox,* and even Sewell and Rutty's histories of the Quakers. He was fond of putting into my hands books which exhibited men of energy and resource in unusual circumstances, struggling against difficulties and overcoming them; of such works I remember Beaver's *African Memoranda* and Collins' *Account of the First Settlement of New South Wales.* Two books which I never wearied of reading were Anson's *Voyages,* so delightful to most young persons, and a collection (Hawkesworth's, I believe) of *Voyages round the World,* in four volumes, beginning with Drake and ending with Cook and Bougainville. Of children's books, any more than of playthings, I had scarcely any, except an occasional gift from a relation or acquaintance; among those I had, *Robinson Crusoe* was pre-eminent and continued to delight me through all my boyhood. It was no part, however, of my father's system to exclude books of amusement, though he allowed them very sparingly. Of such books he possessed at that time next to none, but he borrowed several for me; those which I remember are the *Arabian Nights,* Cazotte's *Arabian Tales, Don Quixote,* Miss Edgeworth's *Popular Tales,* and a book of some reputation in its day, Brooke's *Fool of Quality.*

In my eighth year I commenced learning Latin in conjunction with a younger sister, to whom I taught it as I went on and who afterwards repeated the lessons to my father; and from this time, other sisters and brothers being successively added as pupils, a considerable part of my day's work consisted of this preparatory teaching. It was a part which I greatly disliked, the more so as I was held responsible for the lessons of my pupils in almost as full a sense as for my own; I, however, derived from this discipline the great advantage of learning more thoroughly and retaining more lastingly the things which I was set to teach; perhaps, too, the practice it afforded in explaining difficulties to others may even at that age have been useful. In other respects the experience of my boyhood is not favourable to the plan of teaching children by means of one another.[4] The teaching, I am sure, is very inefficient as teaching, and I well know that the relation between teacher and taught is not a good moral discipline to either. I went in this manner through the Latin grammar and a considerable part of Cornelius Nepos and Caesar's *Commentaries*, but afterwards added to the superintendence of these lessons much longer ones of my own.

In the same year in which I began Latin I made my first commencement in the Greek poets with the *Iliad*. After I had made some progress in this my father put Pope's translation into my hands. It was the first English verse I had cared to read, and it became one of the books in which for many years I most delighted; I think I must have read it from twenty to thirty times through. I should not have thought it worth while to mention a

[4] Mill may have had in mind the monitorial systems of Bell and Lancaster, which were widely used in nineteenth-century England as a cheap and supposedly efficient means of educating the masses.—F. W. G.

taste apparently so natural to boyhood, if I had not, as I think, observed that the keen enjoyment of this brilliant specimen of narrative and versification is not so universal with boys as I should have expected both *a priori* and from my individual experience. Soon after this time I commenced Euclid and somewhat later Algebra, still under my father's tuition.

From my eighth to my twelfth year the Latin books which I remember reading were the *Bucolics* of Virgil and the first six books of the *Aeneid;* all Horace except the *Epodes;* the *Fables* of Phaedrus; the first five books of Livy (to which from my love of the subject I voluntarily added in my hours of leisure the remainder of the first decade); all Sallust; a considerable part of Ovid's *Metamorphoses;* some plays of Terence; two or three books of Lucretius; several of the orations of Cicero and of his writings on oratory; also his letters to Atticus, my father taking the trouble to translate to me from the French the historical explanations in Mingault's[5] notes. In Greek I read the *Iliad* and *Odyssey* through; one or two plays of Sophocles, Euripides and Aristophanes, though by these I profited little; all Thucydides; the *Hellenics* of Xenophon; a great part of Demosthenes, Aeschines and Lysias; Theocritus; Anacreon; part of the *Anthology;* a little of Dionysius; several books of Polybius; and lastly Aristotle's *Rhetoric,* which, as the first expressly scientific treatise on any moral or psychological subject which I had read and containing many of the best observations of the ancients on human nature and life, my father made me study with peculiar care and throw the matter of it into synoptic tables. During the

[5] It is spelled thus in the 1873 edition of the *Autobiography,* in the Oxford World's Classics edition, and in Cavenagh, but the British Museum Catalogue has Mongault.—F. W. G.

same years I learnt elementary geometry and algebra thoroughly, the differential calculus and other portions of the higher mathematics far from thoroughly; for my father, not having kept up this part of his early acquired knowledge, could not spare time to qualify himself for removing my difficulties and left me to deal with them, with little other aid than that of books, while I was continually incurring his displeasure by my inability to solve difficult problems for which he did not see that I had not the necessary previous knowledge.

As to my private reading, I can only speak of what I remember. History continued to be my strongest predilection, and most of all ancient history. Mitford's *Greece* I read continually; my father had put me on my guard against the Tory prejudices of this writer and his perversions of facts for the whitewashing of despots and blackening of popular institutions. These points he discoursed on, exemplifying them from the Greek orators and historians with such effect that in reading Mitford my sympathies were always on the contrary side to those of the author and I could to some extent have argued the point against him; yet this did not diminish the ever new pleasure with which I read the book. Roman history, both in my old favourite, Hooke, and in Ferguson, continued to delight me. A book which, in spite of what is called the dryness of its style, I took great pleasure in was the *Ancient Universal History,* through the incessant reading of which I had my head full of historical details concerning the obscurest ancient people, while about modern history, except detached passages such as the Dutch War of Independence,[6] I knew and cared comparatively little. A voluntary exercise, to

[6] Against Philip II of Spain in the latter half of the sixteenth century.—F. W. G.

which throughout my boyhood I was much addicted, was what I called writing histories. I successively composed a Roman History, picked out of Hooke, an abridgement of the *Ancient Universal History,* a History of Holland, from my favourite Watson and from an anonymous compilation, and in my eleventh and twelfth year I occupied myself with writing what I flattered myself was something serious. This was no less than a history of the Roman Government, compiled (with the assistance of Hooke) from Livy and Dionysius, of which I wrote as much as would have made an octavo volume, extending to the epoch of the Licinian Laws.[7] It was, in fact, an account of the struggles between the patricians and plebeians, which now engrossed all the interest in my mind which I had previously felt in the mere wars and conquests of the Romans. I discussed all the constitutional points as they arose; though quite ignorant of Niebuhr's researches I, by such lights as my father had given me, vindicated the Agrarian Laws on the evidence of Livy and upheld to the best of my ability the Roman democratic party. A few years later, in my contempt of my childish efforts, I destroyed all these papers, not then anticipating that I could ever feel any curiosity about my first attempts at writing and reasoning. My father encouraged me in this useful amusement, though, as I

[7] In 367 B.C. the tribunes C. Licinius Stolo and L. Sextius carried a law which regulated the amount of public land that could be held by any one person, thus freeing excess land for distribution among the poorer citizens of Rome. This and other agrarian laws were a part of the struggle between the nobles (patricians) and the ordinary citizens (plebeians), in which the latter sought to establish their political and economic security. The German historian Barthold Georg Niebuhr, to whom Mill refers below, established by the methods and the extent of his researches a new conception of historical scholarship; his *Römische Geschichte* was published between 1811 and 1832.—F. W. G.

think judiciously, he never asked to see what I wrote, so that I did not feel that in writing it I was accountable to anyone nor had the chilling sensation of being under a critical eye.

But though these exercises in history were never a compulsory lesson, there was another kind of composition which was so, namely, writing verses, and it was one of the most disagreeable of my tasks. Greek and Latin verses I did not write, nor learnt the prosody of those languages. My father, thinking this not worth the time it required, contented himself with making me read aloud to him and correcting false quantities. I never composed at all in Greek, even in prose, and but little in Latin. Not that my father could be indifferent to the value of this practice in giving a thorough knowledge of these languages, but because there really was not time for it. The verses I was required to write were English. When I first read Pope's Homer, I ambitiously attempted to compose something of the same kind and achieved as much as one book of a continuation of the *Iliad*. There, probably, the spontaneous promptings of my poetical ambition would have stopped; but the exercise, begun from choice, was continued by command. Conformably to my father's usual practice of explaining to me, as far as possible, the reasons for what he required me to do, he gave me for this, as I well remember, two reasons highly characteristic of him; one was that some things could be expressed better and more forcibly in verse than in prose; this, he said, was a real advantage. The other was that people in general attached more value to verse than it deserved, and the power of writing it was on this account worth acquiring. He generally left me to choose my own subjects, which, as far as I remember, were mostly addresses to some mythological personage or allegorical abstraction; but he made me translate into English verse many of Horace's shorter poems; I also remember his giving me Thomson's *Winter* to read and afterwards making me attempt (without book) to write something myself on the same subject. The verses I wrote were, of course, the merest rubbish, nor did I ever attain any facility of versification, but the practice may have been useful in making it easier for me at a later period to acquire readiness of expression.* I had read up to this time very little English poetry. Shakespeare my father had put into my hands, chiefly for the sake of the historical plays, from which, however, I went on to the others. My father never was a great admirer of Shakespeare, the English idolatry of whom he used to attack with some severity. He cared little for any English poetry except Milton (for whom he had the highest admiration), Goldsmith, Burns, and Gray's *Bard,* which he preferred to his *Elegy;* perhaps I may add Cowper and Beattie. He had some value for Spenser, and I remember his reading to me (unlike his usual practice of making me read to him) the first book of the *Fairie Queene;* but I took little pleasure in it. The poetry of the present century he saw scarcely any merit in, and I hardly became acquainted with any of it till I was grown up to manhood, except the metrical romances of Walter Scott,[8] which I read at his recommendation and was intensely

* In a subsequent stage of boyhood, when these exercises had ceased to be compulsory, like most youthful writers I wrote tragedies, under the inspiration not so much of Shakespeare as of Joanna Baillie, whose *Constantine Paleologus* in particular appeared to me one of the most glorious of human compositions. I still think it one of the best dramas of the last two centuries.—J. S. M.

[8] Such as *The Lay of the Last Minstrel, Marmion,* and *The Lady of the Lake.*—F. W. G.

delighted with—as I always was with animated narrative. Dryden's Poems were among my father's books, and many of these he made me read, but I never cared for any of them except *Alexander's Feast,* which, as well as many of the songs in Walter Scott, I used to sing internally to a music of my own; to some of the latter, indeed, I went so far as to compose airs, which I still remember. Cowper's short poems I read with some pleasure, but never got far into the longer ones; and nothing in the two volumes interested me like the prose account of his three hares.[9] In my thirteenth year I met with Campbell's poems, among which *Lochiel, Hohenlinden, The Exile of Erin* and some others gave me sensations I had never before experienced from poetry. Here, too, I made nothing of the longer poems except the striking opening of *Gertrude of Wyoming,* which long kept its place in my feelings as the perfection of pathos.

During this part of my childhood one of my greatest amusements was experimental science—in the theoretical, however, not the practical sense of the word; not trying experiments—a kind of discipline which I have often regretted not having had—nor even seeing, but merely reading about them. I never remember being so wrapt up in any book as I was in Joyce's *Scientific Dialogues;* and I was rather recalcitrant to my father's criticisms of the bad reasoning respecting the first principles of physics which abounds in the early part of that work. I devoured treatises on chemistry, especially that of my father's early friend and schoolfellow, Dr. Thom-

[9] This he wrote in a letter to *The Gentleman's Magazine,* June 1784. The hares were given to him when he was convalescing from an attack of mental disorder, and looking after them greatly helped his recovery. Their names were Bess, Puss, and Tiney (all males, nevertheless); on the death of Tiney in 1783 he wrote the delightful *Epitaph on a Hare.*—F. W. G.

son, for years before I attended a lecture or saw an experiment.

From about the age of twelve I entered into another and more advanced stage in my course of instruction, in which the main object was no longer the aids and appliances of thought, but the thoughts themselves. This commenced with logic, in which I began at once with the *Organon* and read it to the *Analytics* inclusive, but profited little by the *Posterior Analytics,* which belong to a branch of speculation I was not yet ripe for.[10] Contemporaneously with the *Organon* my father made me read the whole or parts of several of the Latin treatises on the scholastic logic, giving each day to him in our walks a minute account of what I had read and answering his numerous and searching questions. After this I went in a similar manner through the *Computatio sive Logica* of Hobbes, a work of a much higher order of thought than the books of the school logicians, and which he estimated very highly—in my own opinion beyond its merits, great as these are. It was his invariable practice, whatever studies he exacted from me, to make me as far as possible understand and feel the utility of them; and this he deemed peculiarly fitting in the case of the syllogistic logic, the usefulness of which had been impugned by so many writers of authority. I well remember how, and in what particular walk in the neighbourhood of Bagshot Heath (where we were on a visit to his old friend Mr. Wallace, then one of the Mathematical Professors at Sandhurst), he first attempted by questions to make me think on the subject and frame some conception of what constituted the utility of the syllogistic

[10] The *Organon* ("instrument", "tool"—of thought) is the collective name of Aristotle's logical works which include the *Analytics* and *Posterior Analytics.*—F. W. G.

logic, and when I failed in this, to make me understand it by explanations. The explanations did not make the matter at all clear to me at the time, but they were not therefore useless; they remained as a nucleus for my observations and reflections to crystallise upon, the import of his general remarks being interpreted to me by the particular instances which came under my notice afterwards. My own consciousness and experience ultimately led me to appreciate quite as highly as he did the value of an early practical familiarity with the school logic. I know of nothing in my education to which I think myself more indebted for whatever capacity of thinking I have attained. The first intellectual operation in which I arrived at any proficiency was dissecting a bad argument and finding in what part the fallacy lay; and though whatever capacity of this sort I attained was due to the fact that it was an intellectual exercise in which I was most perseveringly drilled by my father, yet it is also true that the school logic and the mental habits acquired in studying it were among the principal instruments of this drilling. I am persuaded that nothing in modern education tends so much, when properly used, to form exact thinkers, who attach a precise meaning to words and propositions and are not imposed on by vague, loose or ambiguous terms.[11] The boasted influence of mathematical studies is nothing to it; for in mathematical processes none of the real difficulties of correct ratiocination occur. It is also a study peculiarly adapted to an early stage in the education of philosophical students, since it does not presuppose the slow process of acquiring by experience and reflection valuable thoughts of their own. They may become capable of

[11] Cf. *Inaugural Address,* pp. 193–197.—F. W. G.

disentangling the intricacies of confused and self-contradictory thought before their own thinking faculties are much advanced—a power which, for want of some such discipline, many otherwise able men altogether lack and, when they have to answer opponents, only endeavour by such arguments as they can command to support the opposite conclusion, scarcely even attempting to confute the reasonings of their antagonists and therefore at the utmost leaving the question, as far as it depends on argument, a balanced one.

During this time the Latin and Greek books which I continued to read with my father were chiefly such as were worth studying, not for the language merely, but also for the thoughts. This included much of the orators and especially Demosthenes, some of whose principal orations I read several times over and wrote out, by way of exercise, a full analysis of them. My father's comments on these orations when I read them to him were very instructive to me. He not only drew my attention to the insight they afforded into Athenian institutions and the principles of legislation and government which they often illustrated, but pointed out the skill and art of the orator: how everything important to his purpose was said at the exact moment when he had brought the minds of his audience into the state most fitted to receive it; how he made steal into their minds gradually and by insinuation thoughts which, if expressed in a more direct manner, would have roused their opposition. Most of these reflections were beyond my capacity of full comprehension at the time; but they left seed behind which germinated in due season. At this time I also read the whole of Tacitus, Juvenal and Quintilian. The latter, owing to his obscure style and to the scholastic details of which many parts of his treatise are made up, is little read and seldom sufficiently appreciated. His book is a kind of encyclopaedia of the thoughts of the ancients on the whole field of education and culture; and I have retained through life many valuable ideas which I can distinctly trace to my reading of him even at that early age. It was at this period that I read for the first time some of the most important dialogues of Plato, in particular the *Gorgias,* the *Protagoras* and the *Republic.* There is no author to whom my father thought himself more indebted for his own mental culture than Plato, or whom he more frequently recommended to young students. I can bear similar testimony in regard to myself. The Socratic method, of which the Platonic dialogues are the chief example, is unsurpassed as a discipline for correcting the errors and clearing up the confusions incident to the *intellectus sibi permissus,*[12] the understanding which has made up all its bundles of associations[13] under the guidance of popular phraseology. The close, searching *elenchus*[14] by which the man of vague generalities is constrained either to express his meaning to himself in definite terms or to confess that he does not know what he is talking about; the perpetual testing of all general statements by particular instances; the siege in form which is laid to the meaning of large abstract terms by fixing upon some still larger class-name which includes that and more and dividing down to the thing sought, marking out its limits and definition by a series of accurately drawn distinctions between it and each of

[12] Literally "the mind left to itself."—F. W. G.

[13] For Mill's association psychology, see the Introduction, pp. 19–21.—F. W. G.

[14] *Elenchus* is a Greek word meaning "test" or "scrutiny," especially with a view to refutation. On this see also *Inaugural Address,* pp. 176–177, and Mill's review of Grote's *Plato* in *Dissertations and Discussions,* III (London, 1867), 320 ff.—F. W. G.

the cognate objects which are successively parted off from it; all this as an education for precise thinking is inestimable, and all this, even at that age, took such hold of me that it became part of my own mind. I have felt ever since that the title of Platonist belongs by far better right to those who have been nourished in, and have endeavoured to practise, Plato's mode of investigation than to those who are distinguished only by the adoption of certain dogmatical conclusions drawn mostly from the least intelligible of his works and which the character of his mind and writings makes it uncertain whether he himself regarded as anything more than poetic fancies or philosophic conjectures.

In going through Plato and Demosthenes, since I could now read these authors as far as the language was concerned with perfect ease, I was not required to construe them sentence by sentence but to read them aloud to my father, answering questions when he asked; but the particular attention which he paid to elocution (in which his own excellence was remarkable) made this reading aloud to him a most painful task. Of all things which he required me to do there was none which I did so constantly ill or in which he so perpetually lost his temper with me. He had thought much on the principles of the art of reading, especially the most neglected part of it, the inflections of the voice or *modulation,* as writers on elocution call it (in contrast with *articulation* on the one side and *expression* on the other), and had reduced it to rules grounded on the logical analysis of a sentence. These rules he strongly impressed upon me and took me severely to task for every violation of them; but I even then remarked (though I did not venture to make the remark to him) that though he reproached me when I read a sentence ill and *told* me how I ought to have read it, he never, by reading it himself, *showed* me how it ought to be read. A defect running through his otherwise admirable modes of instruction, as it did through all his modes of thought, was that of trusting too much to the intelligibleness of the abstract when not embodied in the concrete. It was at a much later period of my youth, when practising elocution by myself or with companions of my own age, that I for the first time understood the object of his rules and saw the psychological grounds of them. At that time I and others followed out the subject into its ramifications and could have composed a very useful treatise grounded on my father's principles. He himself left those principles and rules unwritten. I regret that when my mind was full of the subject from systematic practice I did not put them and our improvements of them into a formal shape.

A book which contributed largely to my education, in the best sense of the term, was my father's *History of India.* It was published in the beginning of 1818. During the year previous, while it was passing through the press, I used to read the proof sheets to him; or rather, I read the manuscript to him while he corrected the proofs. The number of new ideas which I received from this remarkable book and the impulse and stimulus as well as guidance given to my thoughts by its criticisms and disquisitions on society and civilisation in the Hindoo part, on institutions and the acts of governments in the English part, made my early familiarity with it eminently useful to my subsequent progress. And though I can perceive deficiencies in it now compared with a perfect standard, I still think it, if not the most, one of the most instructive histories ever written and one of the books from which most benefit may be derived by a mind in the course of making up its opinions.

The Preface, among the most characteristic of my father's writings as well as the richest in materials of thought, gives a picture which may be entirely depended on of the sentiments and expectations with which he wrote the *History*. Saturated as the book is with the opinions and modes of judgement of a democratic radicalism then regarded as extreme, and treating with a severity at that time most unusual the English Constitution, the English law and all parties and classes who possessed any considerable influence in the country, he may have expected reputation but certainly not advancement in life from its publication; nor could he have supposed that it would raise up anything but enemies for him in powerful quarters; least of all could he have expected favour from the East India Company,[15] to whose commercial privileges he was unqualifiedly hostile, and on the acts of whose government he had made so many severe comments; though in various parts of the book he bore a testimony in their favour which he felt to be their just due, namely, that no Government had on the whole given so much proof, to the extent of its lights, of good intention towards its subjects, and that if the acts of any other Government had the light of publicity as completely let in upon them, they would in all probability still less bear scrutiny.

On learning, however, in the spring of 1819, about a year after the publication of the *History*, that the East India Directors desired to strengthen the part of their home establishment which was employed in carrying on the correspondence with India, my father declared himself a candidate for that employment and, to the credit of the Directors, successfully. He was appointed one of

[15] By whom, as we are told in the next paragraph, James Mill was later employed.—F. W. G.

the Assistants of the Examiner of India Correspondence, officers whose duty it was to prepare drafts of despatches to India for consideration by the Directors in the principal departments of administration. In this office and in that of Examiner, which he subsequently attained, the influence which his talents, his reputation and his decision of character gave him with superiors who really desired the good government of India enabled him to a great extent to throw into his drafts of despatches, and to carry through the ordeal of the Court of Directors and Board of Control without having their force much weakened, his real opinions on Indian subjects. In his *History* he had set forth for the first time many of the true principles of Indian administration, and his despatches, following his *History,* did more than had ever been done before to promote the improvement of India and teach Indian officials to understand their business. If a selection of them were published, they would, I am convinced, place his character as a practical statesman fully on a level with his eminence as a speculative writer.

This new employment of his time caused no relaxation in his attention to my education. It was in this same year, 1819, that he took me through a complete course of political economy. His loved and intimate friend, Ricardo, had shortly before published the book which formed so great an epoch in political economy, a book which never would have been published or written but for the entreaty and strong encouragement of my father;[16] for Ricardo, the most modest of men, though firmly convinced of the truth of his doctrines, deemed himself so little capable of doing them justice in exposition and expression, that he shrank from the idea of

[16] *Principles of Political Economy and Taxation* (1817); see p. 147 below.—F. W. G.

publicity. The same friendly encouragement induced Ricardo a year or two later to become a member of the House of Commons, where, during the few remaining years of his life (unhappily cut short in the full vigour of his intellect) he rendered so much service to his and my father's opinions both on political economy and on other subjects.

Though Ricardo's great work was already in print, no didactic treatise embodying its doctrines in a manner fit for learners had yet appeared. My father, therefore, commenced instructing me in the science by a sort of lectures, which he delivered to me in our walks. He expounded each day a portion of the subject and I gave him next day a written account of it, which he made me rewrite over and over again until it was clear, precise and tolerably complete. In this manner I went through the whole extent of the science, and the written outline of it which resulted from my daily *compte rendu* served him afterwards as notes from which to write his *Elements of Political Economy*.[17] After this I read Ricardo, giving an account daily of what I read and discussing in the best manner I could the collateral points which offered themselves in our progress.

On money, as the most intricate part of the subject, he made me read in the same manner Ricardo's admirable pamphlets, written during what was called the bullion controversy;[18] to these succeeded Adam Smith; and in this reading it was one of my father's main objects to make me apply to Smith's more superficial view of political economy the superior lights of Ricardo and detect what was fallacious in Smith's arguments or erroneous in any of his conclusions. Such a mode of instruc-

[17] Published 1821.—F. W. G.

[18] See p. 147.—F. W. G.

tion was excellently calculated to form a thinker; but it required to be worked by a thinker as close and vigorous as my father. The path was a thorny one even to him, and I am sure it was so to me, notwithstanding the strong interest I took in the subject. He was often, and much beyond reason, provoked by my failures in cases where success could not have been expected; but in the main his method was right, and it succeeded. I do not believe that any scientific teaching ever was more thorough or better fitted for training the faculties than the mode in which logic and political economy were taught to me by my father. Striving, even in an exaggerated degree, to call forth the activity of my faculties by making me find out everything for myself, he gave his explanations not before but after I had felt the full force of the difficulties, and not only gave me an accurate knowledge of these two great subjects, as far as they were then understood, but made me a thinker on both. I thought for myself almost from the first and occasionally thought differently from him, though for a long time only on minor points and making his opinion the ultimate standard. At a later period I even occasionally convinced him and altered his opinion on some points of detail—which I state to his honour, not my own. It at once exemplifies his perfect candour and the real worth of his method of teaching.

At this point concluded what can properly be called my lessons; when I was about fourteen I left England for more than a year and after my return, though my studies went on under my father's general direction, he was no longer my schoolmaster. I shall therefore pause here and turn back to matters of a more general nature connected with the part of my life and education included in the preceding reminiscences.

In the course of instruction which I have partially retraced the point most superficially apparent is the great effort to give during the years of childhood an amount of knowledge in what are considered the higher branches of education which is seldom acquired (if acquired at all) until the age of manhood. The result of the experiment shows the ease with which this may be done, and places in a strong light the wretched waste of so many precious years as are spent in acquiring the modicum of Latin and Greek commonly taught to schoolboys[19]—a waste which has led so many educational reformers to entertain the ill-judged proposal of discarding these languages altogether from general education. If I had been by nature extremely quick of apprehension or had possessed a very accurate and retentive memory or were of a remarkably active and energetic character, the trial would not be conclusive; but in all these natural gifts I am rather below than above par;[20] what I could do could assuredly be done by any boy or girl of average capacity and healthy physical constitution; and if I have accomplished anything, I owe it, among other fortunate circumstances, to the fact that through the early training bestowed on me by my father I started, I may fairly say, with an advantage of a quarter of a century over my contemporaries.

There was one cardinal point in this training of which I have already given some indication and which, more than anything else, was the cause of whatever good it effected. Most boys or youths who have had much knowledge drilled into them have their mental capacities, not

[19] Cf. *Inaugural Address,* pp. 160 ff. and note.—F. W. G.

[20] Mill clearly underestimates his own abilities, which, even without his remarkable education, would surely have raised him to eminence.—F. W. G.

strengthened, but overlaid by it.[21] They are crammed with mere facts and with the opinions or phrases of other people, and these are accepted as a substitute for the power to form opinions of their own; and thus the sons of eminent fathers, who have spared no pains in their education, so often grow up mere parroters of what they have learnt, incapable of using their minds except in the furrows traced for them. Mine, however, was not an education of cram. My father never permitted anything which I learnt to degenerate into a mere exercise of memory. He strove to make the understanding not only go along with every step of the teaching but, if possible, precede it. Anything which could be found out by thinking I never was told until I had exhausted my efforts to find it out for myself. As far as I can trust my remembrance, I acquitted myself very lamely in this department; my recollection of such matters is almost wholly of failures, hardly ever of success. It is true the failures were often in things in which success in so early a stage of my progress was almost impossible. I remember at some time in my thirteenth year, on my happening to use the word "idea", he asked me what an idea was and expressed some displeasure at my ineffectual efforts to define the word; I recollect also his indignation at my using the common expression that something was true in theory but required correction in practice; and how, after making me vainly strive to define the word "theory", he explained its meaning and showed the fallacy of the vulgar form of speech which I had used, leaving me fully persuaded that in being unable to give a correct definition of "theory" and in speaking of it as something

[21] In his essay *On Genius* (1832), Mill contrasts "cramming" with the kind of education that promotes originality. Cf. *Inaugural Address*, p. 156.—F. W. G.

which might be at variance with practice I had shown unparalleled ignorance. In this he seems, and perhaps was, very unreasonable, but, I think, only in being angry at my failure. A pupil from whom nothing is ever demanded which he cannot do never does all he can.

One of the evils most liable to attend on any sort of early proficiency, and which often fatally blights its promise, my father most anxiously guarded against. This was self-conceit. He kept me with extreme vigilance out of the way of hearing myself praised or of being led to make self-flattering comparisons between myself and others. From his own intercourse with me I could derive none but a very humble opinion of myself; and the standard of comparison he always held up to me was not what other people did, but what a man could and ought to do. He completely succeeded in preserving me from the sort of influences he so much dreaded. I was not at all aware that my attainments were anything unusual at my age. If I accidentally had my attention drawn to the fact that some other boy knew less than myself—which happened less often than might be imagined—I concluded, not that I knew much, but that he, for some reason or other, knew little or that his knowledge was of a different kind from mine. My state of mind was not humility, but neither was it arrogance. I never thought of saying to myself, I am or I can do so and so. I neither estimated myself highly nor lowly; I did not estimate myself at all. If I thought anything about myself, it was that I was rather backward in my studies, since I always found myself so in comparison with what my father expected from me. I assert this with confidence, though it was not the impression of various persons who saw me in my childhood. They, as I have since found, thought me greatly and disagreeably self-conceited, probably because I was disputatious and did not scruple to give direct contradictions to things which I heard said. I suppose I acquired this bad habit from having been encouraged in an unusual degree to talk on matters beyond my age and with grown persons, while I never had inculcated on me the usual respect for them. My father did not correct this ill-breeding and impertinence, probably from not being aware of it, for I was always too much in awe of him to be otherwise than extremely subdued and quiet in his presence. Yet with all this I had no notion of any superiority in myself; and well was it for me that I had not. I remember the very place in Hyde Park where, in my fourteenth year, on the eve of leaving my father's house for a long absence, he told me that I should find, as I got acquainted with new people, that I had been taught many things which youths of my age did not commonly know, and that many persons would be disposed to talk to me of this and to compliment me upon it. What other things he said on this topic I remember very imperfectly; but he wound up by saying that whatever I knew more than others could not be ascribed to any merit in me but to the very unusual advantage which had fallen to my lot of having a father who was able to teach me and willing to give the necessary trouble and time; that it was no matter of praise to me if I knew more than those who had not had a similar advantage, but the deepest disgrace to me if I did not. I have a distinct remembrance that the suggestion thus for the first time made to me, that I knew more than other youths who were considered well educated, was to me a piece of information to which, as to all other things which my father told me, I gave implicit credence, but which did not at all impress me as a personal matter. I felt no disposition to glorify myself upon the circumstance that there were other persons who did not know what I knew; nor had I ever flattered myself that my acquirements, whatever they might be, were any merit of mine; but now, when my attention was called to the subject, I felt that what my father had said respecting my peculiar advantages was exactly the truth and common sense of the matter, and it fixed my opinion and feeling from that time forward.

It is evident that this, among many other of the purposes of my father's scheme of education, could not have been accomplished if he had not carefully kept me from having any great amount of intercourse with other boys. He was earnestly bent upon my escaping not only the corrupting influence which boys exercise over boys, but the contagion of vulgar modes of thought and feeling; and for this he was willing that I should pay the price of inferiority in the accomplishments which schoolboys in all countries chiefly cultivate. The deficiencies in my education were principally in the things which boys learn from being turned out to shift for themselves and from being brought together in large numbers. From temperance and much walking I grew up healthy and hardy, though not muscular; but I could do no feats of skill or physical strength, and knew none of the ordinary bodily exercises. It was not that play or time for it was refused me. Though no holidays were allowed, lest the habit of work should be broken and a taste for idleness acquired, I had ample leisure in every day to amuse myself; but as I had no boy companions and the animal need of physical activity was satisfied by walking, my amusements, which were mostly solitary, were in general of a quiet if not a bookish turn and gave little stimulus to any other kind even of mental activity than that which was already called forth by my studies. I consequently remained long, and in a less degree have always remained, inexpert in anything requiring manual dexterity;[22] my mind, as well as my hands, did its work very lamely when it was applied, or ought to have been applied, to the practical details which, as they are the chief interest of life to the majority of men, are also the things in which whatever mental capacity they have shows itself. I was constantly meriting reproof by inattention, inobservance and general slackness of mind in matters of daily life. My father was the extreme opposite in these particulars; his senses and mental faculties were always on the alert; he carried decision and energy of character in his whole manner and into every action of life; and this, as much as his talents, contributed to the strong impression which he always made upon those with whom he came into personal contact. But the children of energetic parents frequently grow up unenergetic, because they lean on their parents and the parents are energetic for them. The education which my father gave me was in itself much more fitted for training me to *know* than to *do*. Not that he was unaware of my deficiencies; both as a boy and as a youth I was incessantly smarting under his severe admonitions on the subject. There was anything but insensibility[23] or tolerance on his part towards such shortcomings; but, while he saved me from the demoralising effects of school life, he made no effort to provide me with any sufficient substitute for its practicalising influences. Whatever qualities he himself, probably, had acquired without difficulty or special training he seems to have supposed that I

[22] Mill's practical ineptitude is suggested in Packe's *Life of John Stuart Mill*, pp. 361–364, where he has to cope with domestic matters in his wife's absence.—F. W. G.

[23] "Indifference."—F. W. G.

ought to acquire as easily. He had not, I think, bestowed the same amount of thought and attention on this as on most other branches of education; and here, as well [as] in some other points of my tuition, he seems to have expected effects without causes.

II

Moral Influences in Early Youth. My Father's Character and Opinions

In my education, as in that of everyone, the moral influences, which are so much more important than all others, are also the most complicated and the most difficult to specify with any approach to completeness. Without attempting the hopeless task of detailing the circumstances by which in this respect my early character may have been shaped, I shall confine myself to a few leading points which form an indispensable part of any true account of my education.

I was brought up from the first without any religious belief in the ordinary acceptation of the term. My father, educated in the creed of Scotch Presbyterianism, had by his own studies and reflections been early led to reject not only the belief in revelation, but the foundations of what is commonly called natural religion. I have heard him say that the turning point of his mind on the subject was reading Butler's *Analogy*.[24] That work, of which he always continued to speak with respect, kept him, as he said, for some considerable time a believer in the divine authority of Christianity by proving to him that, whatever are the difficulties in believing

[24] Joseph Butler (1692–1752), bishop of Bristol and later of Durham; the *Analogy* is a defense of revealed religion.—F. W. G.

that the Old and New Testament proceed from or record the acts of a perfectly wise and good being, the same and still greater difficulties stand in the way of the belief that a being of such a character can have been the Maker of the universe. He considered Butler's argument as conclusive against the only opponents for whom it was intended. Those who admit an omnipotent as well as perfectly just and benevolent maker and ruler of such a world as this can say little against Christianity but what can, with at least equal force, be retorted against themselves. Finding, therefore, no halting place in Deism he remained in a state of perplexity until, doubtless after many struggles, he yielded to the conviction that concerning the origin of things nothing whatever can be known. This is the only correct statement of his opinion, for dogmatic atheism he looked upon as absurd, as most of those whom the world has considered atheists have always done. These particulars are important, because they show that my father's rejection of all that is called religious belief was not, as many might suppose, primarily a matter of logic and evidence; the grounds of it were moral still more than intellectual. He found it impossible to believe that a world so full of evil was the work of an Author combining infinite power with perfect goodness and righteousness. His intellect spurned the subtleties by which men attempt to blind themselves to this open contradiction. The Sabaean or Manichaean[25] theory of a Good and an Evil Principle struggling against each other for the government of the universe he would not have equally condemned; and I have heard him express surprise that no one revived it in our time. He would have regarded it

[25] A Persian religious sect founded by Mani (c. 216–277 A.D.).—F. W. G.

as a mere hypothesis, but he would have ascribed to it no depraving influence. As it was, his aversion to religion, in the sense usually attached to the term, was of the same kind with that of Lucretius:[26] he regarded it with the feelings due not to a mere mental delusion, but to a great moral evil. He looked upon it as the greatest enemy of morality, first, by setting up fictitious excellences—belief in creeds, devotional feelings and ceremonies not connected with the good of human-kind—and causing these to be accepted as substitutes for genuine virtues; but above all by radically vitiating the standard of morals, making it consist in doing the will of a being on whom it lavishes indeed all the phrases of adulation, but whom in sober truth it depicts as eminently hateful. I have a hundred times heard him say that all ages and nations have represented their gods as wicked in a constantly increasing progression, that mankind have gone on adding trait after trait till they reached the most perfect conception of wickedness which the human mind can devise and have called this God and prostrated themselves before it. This *ne plus ultra* of wickedness he considered to be embodied in what is commonly presented to mankind as the creed of Christianity. Think (he used to say) of a being who would make a hell—who would create the human race with the infallible foreknowledge, and therefore with the intention, that the great majority of them were to be consigned to horrible and everlasting torment. The time, I believe, is drawing near when this dreadful conception of an object of worship will no longer be identified with Christianity, and when all persons with any sense of moral good and evil will look upon it with the same indignation with

[26] See the note on Lucretius, p. 138.—F. W. G.

which my father regarded it. My father was as well aware as anyone that Christians do not, in general, undergo the demoralising consequences which seem inherent in such a creed in the manner or to the extent which might have been expected from it. The same slovenliness of thought and subjection of the reason to fears, wishes and affections which enable them to accept a theory involving a contradiction in terms prevents them from perceiving the logical consequences of the theory. Such is the facility with which mankind believe at one and the same time things inconsistent with one another, and so few are those who draw from what they receive as truths any consequences but those recommended to them by their feelings, that multitudes have held the undoubting belief in an omnipotent Author of hell, and have nevertheless identified that being with the best conception they were able to form of perfect goodness. Their worship was not paid to the demon which such a being as they imagined would really be, but to their own ideal of excellence. The evil is that such a belief keeps the ideal wretchedly low and opposes the most obstinate resistance to all thought which has a tendency to raise it higher. Believers shrink from every train of ideas which would lead the mind to a clear conception and an elevated standard of excellence, because they feel (even when they do not distinctly see) that such a standard would conflict with many of the dispensations of nature and with much of what they are accustomed to consider as the Christian creed. And thus morality continues a matter of blind tradition with no consistent principle nor even any consistent feeling to guide it.

It would have been wholly inconsistent with my father's ideas of duty to allow me to acquire impressions contrary to his convictions and feelings respecting religion; and he impressed upon me from the first that the manner in which the world came into existence was a subject on which nothing was known; that the question, "Who made me?" cannot be answered because we have no experience or authentic information from which to answer it; and that any answer only throws the difficulty a step further back, since the question immediately presents itself, "Who made God?" He at the same time took care that I should be acquainted with what had been thought by mankind on these impenetrable problems. I have mentioned at how early an age he made me a reader of ecclesiastical history; and he taught me to take the strongest interest in the Reformation, as the great and decisive contest against priestly tyranny for liberty of thought.

I am thus one of the very few examples in this country of one who has not thrown off religious belief but never had it; I grew up in a negative state with regard to it. I looked upon the modern exactly as I did upon the ancient religion, as something which in no way concerned me. It did not seem to me more strange that English people should believe what I did not than that the men I read of in Herodotus should have done so. History had made the variety of opinions among mankind a fact familiar to me, and this was but a prolongation of that fact. This point in my early education had, however, incidentally one bad consequence deserving notice. In giving me an opinion contrary to that of the world my father thought it necessary to give it as one which could not prudently be avowed to the world. This lesson of keeping my thoughts to myself at that early age was attended with some moral disadvantages, though my limited intercourse with strangers, especially such as were likely to speak to me on religion, prevented me from being placed in the alternative of avowal or hypocrisy. I remember two occasions in my boyhood on which I felt myself in this alternative, and in both cases I avowed my disbelief and defended it. My opponents were boys, considerably older than myself; one of them I certainly staggered at the time, but the subject was never renewed between us; the other, who was surprised and somewhat shocked, did his best to convince me for some time, without effect.

The great advance in liberty of discussion, which is one of the most important differences between the present time and that of my childhood, has greatly altered the moralities of this question; and I think that few men of my father's intellect and public spirit, holding with such intensity of moral conviction as he did unpopular opinions on religion or on any other of the great subjects of thought, would now either practise or inculcate the withholding of them from the world, unless in the cases, becoming fewer every day, in which frankness on these subjects would either risk the loss of means of subsistence or would amount to exclusion from some sphere of usefulness peculiarly suitable to the capacities of the individual. On religion in particular the time appears to me to have come when it is the duty of all who, being qualified in point of knowledge, have on mature consideration satisfied themselves that the current opinions are not only false but hurtful, to make their dissent known; at least, if they are among those whose station or reputation gives their opinion a chance of being attended to. Such an avowal would put an end, at once and for ever, to the vulgar prejudice that what is called, very improperly, unbelief is connected with any bad qualities either of mind or heart. The world would be astonished if it knew how great a proportion of its brightest ornaments—of those most distinguished even in popular estimation for wisdom and virtue—are complete sceptics in religion, many of them refraining from avowal less from personal considerations than from a conscientious, though now in my opinion a most mistaken, apprehension lest by speaking out what would tend to weaken existing beliefs and by consequence (as they suppose) existing restraints, they should do harm instead of good.

Of unbelievers (so called) as well as of believers there are many species, including almost every variety of moral type. But the best among them, as no one who has had opportunities of really knowing them will hesitate to affirm, are more genuinely religious, in the best sense of the word religion, than those who exclusively arrogate to themselves the title. The liberality of the age, or in other words the weakening of the obstinate prejudice which makes men unable to see what is before their eyes because it is contrary to their expectations, has caused it to be very commonly admitted that a deist may be truly religious; but if religion stands for any graces of character and not for mere dogma, the assertion may equally be made of many whose belief is far short of deism. Though they may think the proof incomplete that the universe is a work of design, and though they assuredly disbelieve that it can have an Author and Governor who is *absolute* in power as well as perfect in goodness, they have that which constitutes the principal worth of all religions whatever, an ideal conception of a perfect Being to which they habitually refer as the guide of their conscience; and this ideal of Good is usually far nearer to perfection than the objective Deity of those who think themselves obliged to find absolute goodness in the author of a world so crowded with suffering and so deformed by injustice as ours.

My father's moral convictions, wholly dissevered from religion, were very much of the character of those of the Greek philosophers and were delivered with the force and decision which characterised all that came from him. Even at the very early age at which I read with him the *Memorabilia* of Xenophon I imbibed from that work and from his comments a deep respect for the character of Socrates, who stood in my mind as a model of ideal excellence; and I well remember how my father at that time impressed upon me the lesson of the "Choice of Hercules".[27] At a somewhat later period the lofty moral standard exhibited in the writings of Plato operated upon me with great force. My father's moral inculcations were at all times mainly those of the *"Socratici viri"*:[28] justice, temperance (to which he gave a very extended application), veracity, perseverance, readiness to encounter pain and especially labour; regard for the public good; estimation of persons according to their merits, and of things according to their intrinsic usefulness; a life of exertion in contradiction to one of self-indulgent ease and sloth. These and other moralities he conveyed in brief sentences, uttered as occasion arose, of grave exhortation or stern reprobation and contempt.

But though direct moral teaching does much, indirect does more; and the effect my father produced on my

[27] The fable of the choice of Hercules was invented by the Sophist Prodicus, a contemporary of Socrates. When Hercules was approaching manhood, he was met by two women, Virtue and Vice (who called herself "Joy"). Virtue invited him to a life of unselfish activity, and Vice to a life of pleasure. The interest of the story lay in the speeches of the two women.—F. W. G.

[28] The followers of Socrates.—F. W. G.

character did not depend solely on what he said or did with that direct object, but also, and still more, on what manner of man he was.

In his views of life he partook of the character of the Stoic, the Epicurean and the Cynic, not in the modern but the ancient sense of the word. In his personal qualities the Stoic predominated. His standard of morals was Epicurean inasmuch as it was utilitarian, taking as the exclusive test of right and wrong the tendency of actions to produce pleasure or pain. But he had (and this was the Cynic element) scarcely any belief in pleasure, at least in his later years, of which alone on this point I can speak confidently. He was not insensible to pleasures, but he deemed very few of them worth the price which, at least in the present state of society, must be paid for them. The greater number of miscarriages in life he considered to be attributable to the overvaluing of pleasures. Accordingly, temperance, in the large sense intended by the Greek philosophers—stopping short at the point of moderation in all indulgences—was with him, as with them, almost the central point of educational precept. His inculcations of this virtue fill a large place in my childish remembrances. He thought human life a poor thing at best after the freshness of youth and of unsatisfied curiosity had gone by. This was a topic on which he did not often speak, especially, it may be supposed, in the presence of young persons; but when he did, it was with an air of settled and profound conviction. He would sometimes say that, if life were made what it might be by good government and good education, it would be worth having, but he never spoke with anything like enthusiasm even of that possibility. He never varied in rating intellectual enjoyments above all others, even in value as pleasures, independently of their ulterior benefits. The pleasures of the benevolent affections he placed high in the scale and used to say that he had never known a happy old man, except those who were able to live over again in the pleasures of the young. For passionate emotions of all sorts and for everything which has been said or written in exaltation of them he professed the greatest contempt. He regarded them as a form of madness. "The intense" was with him a bye-word of scornful disapprobation. He regarded as an aberration of the moral standard of modern times, compared with that of the ancients, the great stress laid upon feeling. Feelings as such he considered to be no proper subjects of praise or blame. Right and wrong, good and bad, he regarded as qualities solely of conduct —of acts and omissions—there being no feeling which may not lead and does not frequently lead either to good or to bad actions, conscience itself, the very desire to act right, often leading people to act wrong. Consistently carrying out the doctrine that the object of praise and blame should be the discouragement of wrong conduct and the encouragement of right, he refused to let his praise or blame be influenced by the motive of the agent. He blamed as severely what he thought a bad action, when the motive was a feeling of duty, as if the agents had been consciously evil-doers. He would not have accepted as a plea in mitigation for inquisitors that they sincerely believed burning heretics to be an obligation of conscience. But though he did not allow honesty of purpose to soften his disapprobation of actions, it had its full effect on his estimation of characters. No one prized conscientiousness and rectitude of intention more highly or was more incapable of valuing any person in whom he did not feel assurance of it. But he disliked people quite as much for any other deficiency, provided he thought it equally likely to make them act ill. He disliked, for instance, a fanatic in any bad cause as much or more than one who adopted the same cause from self-interest, because he thought him even more likely to be practically mischievous. And thus his aversion to many intellectual errors, or what he regarded as such, partook, in a certain sense, of the character of a moral feeling. All this is merely saying that he, in a degree once common but now very unusual, threw his feelings into his opinions, which truly it is difficult to understand how any one who possesses much of both can fail to do. None but those who do not care about opinions will confound this with intolerance. Those who, having opinions which they hold to be immensely important and their contraries to be prodigiously hurtful, have any deep regard for the general good, will necessarily dislike, as a class and in the abstract, those who think wrong what they think right and right what they think wrong; though they need not therefore be, nor was my father, insensible to good qualities in an opponent nor governed in their estimation of individuals by one general presumption instead of by the whole of their character. I grant that an earnest person, being no more infallible than other men, is liable to dislike people on account of opinions which do not merit dislike; but if he neither himself does them any ill office nor connives at its being done by others, he is not intolerant; and the forbearance which flows from a conscientious sense of the importance to mankind of the equal freedom of all opinions is the only tolerance which is commendable or, to the highest moral order of minds, possible.

It will be admitted that a man of the opinions and the character above described was likely to leave a strong moral impression on any mind principally formed by him, and that his moral teaching was not likely to err on the side of laxity or indulgence. The element which was chiefly deficient in his moral relation to his children was that of tenderness. I do not believe that this deficiency lay in his own nature. I believe him to have had much more feeling than he habitually showed and much greater capacities of feeling than were ever developed. He resembled most Englishmen in being ashamed of the signs of feeling and, by the absence of demonstration, starving the feelings themselves. If we consider further that he was in the trying position of sole teacher and add to this that his temper was constitutionally irritable, it is impossible not to feel true pity for a father who did and strove to do so much for his children, who would have so valued their affection, yet who must have been constantly feeling that fear of him was drying it up at its source. This was no longer the case later in life and with his younger children. They loved him tenderly; and if I cannot say so much of myself, I was always loyally devoted to him. As regards my own education, I hesitate to pronounce whether I was more a loser or a gainer by his severity. It was not such as to prevent me from having a happy childhood. And I do not believe that boys can be induced to apply themselves with vigour and, what is so much more difficult, perseverance to dry and irksome studies by the sole force of persuasion and soft words. Much must be done and much must be learnt by children for which rigid discipline and known liability to punishment are indispensable as means. It is, no doubt, a very laudable effort in modern teaching to render as much as possible of what the young are required to learn easy and interesting to them. But when this principle is pushed to the length of not requiring them to learn anything *but* what has been made easy and interesting, one of the chief objects of education is sacrificed. I rejoice in the decline of the old brutal and tyrannical system of teaching, which, however, did succeed in enforcing habits of application; but the new, as it seems to me, is training up a race of men who will be incapable of doing anything which is disagreeable to them. I do not, then, believe that fear as an element in education can be dispensed with; but I am sure that it ought not to be the main element; and when it predominates so much as to preclude love and confidence on the part of the child to those who should be the unreservedly trusted advisers of after years, and perhaps to seal up the fountains of frank and spontaneous communicativeness in the child's nature, it is an evil for which a large abatement must be made from the benefits, moral and intellectual, which may flow from any other part of the education.

During this first period of my life the habitual frequenters of my father's house were limited to a very few persons, most of them little known to the world, but whom personal worth and more or less of congeniality with at least his political opinions (not so frequently to be met with then as since) inclined him to cultivate; and his conversations with them I listened to with interest and instruction. My being an habitual inmate of my father's study made me acquainted with the dearest of his friends, David Ricardo, who by his benevolent countenance and kindliness of manner was very attractive to young persons and who, after I became a student of political economy, invited me to his house and to walk with him in order to converse on the subject. I was a more frequent visitor (from about 1817 or 1818) to Mr. Hume,[29] who, born in the same part of Scotland as

[29] Joseph Hume (1777–1855) served as a surgeon in India for the East India Company and later in the British Army; on his return to England in 1808 he turned to politics and for most of the

my father and having been, I rather think, a younger schoolfellow or college companion of his, had on returning from India renewed their youthful acquaintance, and who, coming like many others greatly under the influence of my father's intellect and energy of character, was induced partly by that influence to go into Parliament and there adopt the line of conduct which has given him an honourable place in the history of his country. Of Mr. Bentham I saw much more, owing to the close intimacy which existed between him and my father. I do not know how soon after my father's first arrival in England they became acquainted. But my father was the earliest Englishman[30] of any great mark who thoroughly understood, and in the main adopted, Bentham's general views of ethics, government and law; and this was a natural foundation for sympathy between them and made them familiar companions in a period of Bentham's life during which he admitted much fewer visitors than was the case subsequently. At this time Mr. Bentham passed some part of every year at Barrow Green House in a beautiful part of the Surrey Hills a few miles from Godstone, and there I each summer accompanied my father in a long visit. In 1813 Mr. Bentham, my father and I made an excursion, which included Oxford, Bath and Bristol, Exeter, Plymouth and Portsmouth. In this journey I saw many things which were instructive to me and acquired my first taste for natural scenery in the elementary form of fondness for a "view". In the succeeding winter we moved into a house very near to Mr.

---

rest of his life was a Member of Parliament. He was a leading member of the radical or reforming party and thus had much in common with James Mill (with whom he had been at school in Scotland).—F. W. G.

[30] Strictly a Scot, though English by domicile.—F. W. G.

Bentham's, which my father rented from him, in Queen Square, Westminster. From 1814 to 1817 Mr. Bentham lived during half of each year at Ford Abbey, in Somersetshire (or rather in a part of Devonshire surrounded by Somersetshire), which intervals I had the advantage of passing at that place. This sojourn was, I think, an important circumstance in my education. Nothing contributes more to nourish elevation of sentiments in a people than the large and free character of their habitations. The middle-age architecture, the baronial hall and the spacious and lofty rooms of this fine old place, so unlike the mean and cramped externals of English middle class life, gave the sentiment of a larger and freer existence and were to me a sort of poetic cultivation aided also by the character of the grounds in which the Abbey stood, which were *riant*[31] and secluded, umbrageous, and full of the sound of falling waters.

I owed another of the fortunate circumstances in my education, a year's residence in France, to Mr. Bentham's brother, General Sir Samuel Bentham. I had seen Sir Samuel Bentham and his family at their house near Gosport in the course of the tour already mentioned (he being then Superintendent of the Dockyard at Portsmouth) and during a stay of a few days which they made at Ford Abbey shortly after the peace,[32] before going to live on the Continent. In 1820 they invited me for a six months' visit to them in the South of France, which their kindness ultimately prolonged to nearly a twelve-month. Sir Samuel Bentham, though of a character of mind different from that of his illustrious brother, was a man of very considerable attainments and general powers, with a decided genius for mechanical art. His wife, a daughter

[31] "Gay," "charming."—F. W. G.

[32] After the defeat of Napoleon at Waterloo in 1815.—F. W. G.

of the celebrated chemist, Dr. Fordyce,[33] was a woman of strong will and decided character, much general knowledge and great practical good sense of the Edgeworth kind;[34] she was the ruling spirit of the household, as she deserved, and was well qualified, to be. Their family consisted of one son (the eminent botanist)[35] and three daughters, the youngest about two years my senior. I am indebted to them for much and various instruction and for an almost parental interest in my welfare. When I first joined them, in May, 1820, they occupied the Château of Pompignan (still belonging to a descendant of Voltaire's enemy)[36] on the heights overlooking the plain of the Garonne between Montauban and Toulouse. I accompanied them in an excursion to the Pyrenees, including a stay of some duration at Bagnères de Bigorre, a journey to Pau, Bayonne and Bagnères de Luchon, and an ascent of the Pic du Midi de Bigorre.

This first introduction to the highest order of mountain scenery made the deepest impression on me and gave a colour to my tastes through life. In October we proceeded by the beautiful mountain route of Castres and St. Pons from Toulouse to Montpellier, in which last neighbourhood Sir Samuel had just bought the estate of Restinclière, near the foot of the singular mountain of St. Loup. During this residence in France I acquired a

[33] George Fordyce (1736–1802) was a celebrated physician and lecturer in medical science; he was also a good chemist and mineralogist.—F. W. G.

[34] Maria Edgeworth, the novelist (see the note, p. 144), was a woman of strong practical bent who helped her father in the management of his estate in Ireland.—F. W. G.

[35] George Bentham, one of the greatest of English systematic botanists, president of the Linnaean Society for thirteen years.—F. W. G.

[36] Jean-Jacques le Franc, Marquis de Pompignan (1709–1784).—F. W. G.

familiar knowledge of the French language and acquaintance with the ordinary French literature; I took lessons in various bodily exercises, in none of which, however, I made any proficiency; and at Montpellier I attended the excellent winter courses of lectures at the Faculté des Sciences, those of M. Anglada on chemistry, of M. Provençal on zoology, and of a very accomplished representative of the eighteenth century metaphysics, M. Gergonne, on logic, under the name of Philosophy of the Sciences. I also went through a course of the higher mathematics under the private tuition of M. Lenthéric, a professor at the Lycée of Montpellier. But the greatest, perhaps, of the many advantages which I owed to this episode in my education was that of having breathed for a whole year the free and genial atmosphere of Continental life. This advantage was not the less real though I could not then estimate nor even consciously feel it. Having so little experience of English life, and the few people I knew being mostly such as had public objects of a large and personally disinterested kind at heart, I was ignorant of the low moral tone of what in England is called society: the habit of, not indeed professing, but taking for granted in every mode of implication that conduct is of course always directed towards low and petty objects; the absence of high feelings which manifests itself by sneering depreciation of all demonstrations of them and by general abstinence (except among a few of the stricter religionists) from professing any high principles of action at all, except in those pre-ordained cases in which such profession is put on as part of the costume and formalities of the occasion. I could not then know or estimate the difference between this manner of existence and that of a people like the French, whose faults, if equally real, are at all events different; among whom sentiments which by comparison at least may be called elevated are the current coin of human intercourse both in books and in private life, and though often evaporating in profession are yet kept alive in the nation at large by constant exercise and stimulated by sympathy, so as to form a living and active part of the existence of great numbers of persons and to be recognised and understood by all. Neither could I then appreciate the general culture of the understanding, which results from the habitual exercise of the feelings and is thus carried down into the most uneducated classes of several countries on the Continent in a degree not equalled in England among the so-called educated, except where an unusual tenderness of conscience leads to a habitual exercise of the intellect on questions of right and wrong. I did not know the way in which, among the ordinary English, the absence of interest in things of an unselfish kind, except occasionally in a special thing here and there, and the habit of not speaking to others, nor much even to themselves, about the things in which they do feel interest causes both their feelings and their intellectual faculties to remain undeveloped or to develop themselves only in some single and very limited direction, reducing them, considered as spiritual beings, to a kind of negative existence. All these things I did not perceive till long afterwards; but I even then felt, though without stating it clearly to myself, the contrast between the frank sociability and amiability of French personal intercourse and the English mode of existence in which everybody acts as if everybody else (with few or no exceptions) was either an enemy or a bore. In France, it is true, the bad as well as the good points, both of individual and of national character, come more to the surface and break out more fearlessly in ordinary intercourse than in England;

but the general habit of the people is to show, as well as to expect, friendly feeling in everyone towards every other, wherever there is not some positive cause for the opposite. In England it is only of the best bred people in the upper or upper middle ranks that anything like this can be said.

In my way through Paris, both going and returning, I passed some time in the house of M. Say, the eminent political economist, who was a friend and correspondent of my father, having become acquainted with him on a visit to England a year or two after the peace. He was a man of the later period of the French Revolution, a fine specimen of the best kind of French Republican, one of those who had never bent the knee to Bonaparte, though courted by him to do so—a truly upright, brave and enlightened man. He lived a quiet and studious life, made happy by warm affections, public and private. He was acquainted with many of the chiefs of the Liberal party, and I saw various noteworthy persons while staying at his house, among whom I have pleasure in the recollection of having once seen Saint-Simon,[37] not yet the founder either of a philosophy or a religion, and considered only as a clever *original*. The chief fruit which I carried away from the society I saw was a strong and permanent interest in Continental Liberalism, of which I ever afterwards kept myself *au courant*[38] as much as of English politics—a thing not at all usual in those days with Englishmen, and which had a very salutary influence on my development, keeping me free from the error

[37] Claude Henri, Comte de Saint-Simon (1760–1825), was the founder of French positivist philosophy, of which Auguste Comte was the more celebrated exponent; he served as a volunteer in the American War of Independence against Britain.—F. W. G.

[38] "Currently informed."—F. W. G.

always prevalent in England and from which even my father with all his superiority to prejudice was not exempt, of judging universal questions by a merely English standard. After passing a few weeks at Caen with an old friend of my father's I returned to England in July, 1821, and my education resumed its ordinary course.

III

Last Stage of Education and First of Self-Education

For the first year or two after my visit to France I continued my old studies, with the addition of some new ones. When I returned, my father was just finishing for the press his *Elements of Political Economy,* and he made me perform an exercise on the manuscript which Mr. Bentham practised on all his own writings, making what he called "marginal contents"—a short abstract of every paragraph to enable the writer more easily to judge of, and improve, the order of the ideas and the general character of the exposition. Soon after, my father put into my hands Condillac's *Traité des Sensations* and the logical and metaphysical volumes of his *Cours d'Etudes,*[39] the first (notwithstanding the superficial resemblance between Condillac's psychological system and my father's) quite as much for a warning as for an example. I am not sure whether it was in this winter or the next that I first read a history of the French Revolution. I learnt with astonishment that the principles of democracy, then ap-

[39] Etienne Bonnot de Condillac (1715–1780) was a French philosopher who followed the empiricist doctrines of John Locke, deriving all knowledge from sensation and the mind's own inner "reflection." The *Traité des Sensations* is his chief work; the *Cours d'Etudes* (13 vols., 1769/73) was written for the young duke Ferdinand of Parma, to whom he was tutor.—F. W. G.

parently in so insignificant and hopeless a minority everywhere in Europe, had borne all before them in France thirty years earlier, and had been the creed of the nation. As may be supposed from this, I had previously a very vague idea of that great commotion. I knew only that the French had thrown off the absolute monarchy of Louis XIV and XV, had put the King and Queen to death, guillotined many persons, one of whom was Lavoisier,[40] and had ultimately fallen under the despotism of Bonaparte. From this time, as was natural, the subject took an immense hold of my feelings. It allied itself with all my juvenile aspirations to the character of a democratic champion. What had happened so lately seemed as if it might easily happen again; and the most transcendent glory I was capable of conceiving was that of figuring, successful or unsuccessful, as a Girondist[41] in an English Convention.

During the winter of 1821–2 Mr. John Austin,[42] with whom at the time of my visit to France my father had but lately become acquainted, kindly allowed me to read Roman law with him. My father, notwithstanding his abhorrence of the chaos of barbarism called English Law, had turned his thoughts towards the bar as on the whole less ineligible for me than any other profession; and these readings with Mr. Austin, who had made Bentham's best ideas his own and added much to them from

[40] The celebrated French chemist who demonstrated the role of oxygen in combustion.—F. W. G.

[41] The Girondists were members of the moderate republican party in the French Assembly, 1791–1793; its leaders were the deputies from the Department of the Gironde.—F. W. G.

[42] John Austin later became the first professor of jurisprudence at University College, London (1826–1832); his *Province of Jurisprudence Determined* was published in 1832 and *Lectures on Jurisprudence* posthumously, 1861 to 1863.—F. W. G.

other sources and from his own mind, were not only a valuable introduction to legal studies, but an important portion of general education. With Mr. Austin I read Heineccius on the Institutes, his *Roman Antiquities* and part of his exposition of the Pandects; to which was added a considerable portion of Blackstone.[43] It was at the commencement of these studies that my father, as a needful accompaniment to them, put into my hands Bentham's principal speculations, as interpreted to the Continent, and indeed to all the world, by Dumont in the *Traités de Législation*.[44] The reading of this book was an epoch in my life, one of the turning points in my mental history.

My previous education had been, in a certain sense, already a course of Benthamism. The Benthamic standard of "the greatest happiness" was that which I had always been taught to apply; I was even familiar with an abstract discussion of it, forming an episode in an unpublished dialogue on government written by my father on the Platonic model. Yet in the first pages of Bentham it burst upon me with all the force of novelty. What thus impressed me was the chapter in which Bentham passed judgment on the common modes of reasoning in morals

[43] The *Institutiones Justinianae* was an elementary treatise on Roman law compiled by order of the Emperor Justinian I and published in 533 A.D. "Pandects" was a name given to the *Digest of Justinian*, a collection of passages from the writings of Roman jurists compiled by order of the Emperor and also published in 533. They were extensively studied by a group of German jurists in the later eighteenth and early nineteenth centuries; Heineccius was one of these. On Blackstone, see p. 142.—F. W. G.

[44] Etienne Dumont, a Swiss pastor, acted as editor for Bentham; the *Traités de Legislation* was put together from various manuscripts and published in three volumes in 1802; the first English translation did not appear until 1864. See also p. 46, note.—F. W. G.

and legislation, deduced from phrases like "law of nature", "right reason", "the moral sense", "natural rectitude" and the like, and characterised them as dogmatism in disguise, imposing its sentiments upon others under cover of sounding expressions which convey no reason for the sentiment, but set up the sentiment as its own reason. It had not struck me before that Bentham's principle put an end to all this. The feeling rushed upon me that all previous moralists were superseded and that here indeed was the commencement of a new era in thought. This impression was strengthened by the manner in which Bentham put into scientific form the application of the happiness principle to the morality of actions by analysing the various classes and orders of their consequences. But what struck me at that time most of all was the Classification of Offences, which is much more clear, compact and imposing in Dumont's *rédaction* than in the original work of Bentham from which it was taken. Logic and the dialectics of Plato, which had formed so large a part of my previous training, had given me a strong relish for accurate classification. This taste had been strengthened and enlightened by the study of botany on the principles of what is called the Natural Method, which I had taken up with great zeal, though only as an amusement, during my stay in France;[45] and when I found scientific classification applied to the great and complex subject of Punishable Acts under the guidance of the ethical principle of Pleasurable and Painful Consequences, followed out in the method of detail introduced into these subjects by Bentham, I felt taken up to an eminence from which I

[45] Mill was an enthusiastic amateur botanist and collector of flowers; there are many references to this interest in Packe's *Life of John Stuart Mill*.—F. W. G.

could survey a vast mental domain and see stretching out into the distance intellectual results beyond all computation. As I proceeded further, there seemed to be added to this intellectual clearness the most inspiring prospects of practical improvement in human affairs. To Bentham's general view of the construction of a body of law I was not altogether a stranger, having read with attention that admirable compendium, my father's article on Jurisprudence;[46] but I had read it with little profit and scarcely any interest, no doubt from its extremely general and abstract character and also because it concerned the form more than the substance of the *corpus iuris,* the logic rather than the ethics of law. But Bentham's subject was Legislation, of which Jurisprudence is only the formal part; and at every page he seemed to open a clearer and broader conception of what human opinions and institutions ought to be, how they might be made, what they ought to be, and how far removed from it they now are. When I laid down the last volume of the *Traités,* I had become a different being. The "principle of utility" understood as Bentham understood it and applied in the manner in which he applied it through these three volumes fell exactly into its place as the keystone which held together the detached and fragmentary component parts of my knowledge and beliefs. It gave unity to my conceptions of things. I now had opinions, a creed, a doctrine, a philosophy, in one among the best senses of the word a religion, the inculcation and diffusion of which could be made the principal outward purpose of a life. And I had a grand conception laid before me of changes to be effected in the

[46] This was one of a number of articles which James Mill wrote for the *Encyclopaedia Britannica;* the article on education was also one of these (Introduction, pp. 19, 23).—F. W. G.

condition of mankind through that doctrine. The *Traités de Législation* wound up with what was to me a most impressive picture of human life as it would be made by such opinions and such laws as were recommended in the treatise. The anticipations of practical improvement were studiously moderate, deprecating and discountenancing as reveries of vague enthusiasm many things which will one day seem so natural to human beings, that injustice will probably be done to those who once thought them chimerical. But, in my state of mind, this appearance of superiority to illusion added to the effect which Bentham's doctrines produced on me by heightening the impression of mental power, and the vista of improvement which he did open was sufficiently large and brilliant to light up my life, as well as to give a definite shape to my aspirations.

After this I read from time to time the most important of the other works of Bentham which had then seen the light, either as written by himself or as edited by Dumont. This was my private reading while, under my father's direction, my studies were carried into the higher branches of analytic psychology. I now read Locke's *Essay* and wrote out an account of it consisting of a complete abstract of every chapter with such remarks as occurred to me, which was read by or (I think) to my father and discussed throughout. I performed the same process with Helvetius' *de l'Esprit,* which I read of my own choice. This preparation of abstracts subject to my father's censorship was of great service to me by compelling precision in conceiving and expressing psychological doctrines, whether accepted as truths or only regarded as the opinion of others. After Helvetius my father made me study what he deemed the really master-production in the philosophy of mind, Hartley's *Observations on Man.*

This book, though it did not, like the *Traités de Législation,* give a new colour to my existence, made a very similar impression on me in regard to its immediate subject. Hartley's explanation, incomplete as in many points it is, of the more complex mental phenomena by the law of association commended itself to me at once as a real analysis and made me feel by contrast the insufficiency of the merely verbal generalisations of Condillac and even of the instructive gropings and feelings about for psychological explanations of Locke. It was at this very time that my father commenced writing his *Analysis of Mind,*[47] which carried Hartley's mode of explaining the mental phenomena to so much greater length and depth. He could only command the concentration of thought necessary for this work during the complete leisure of his holiday of a month or six weeks annually; and he commenced it in the summer of 1822 in the first holiday he passed at Dorking, in which neighbourhood from that time to the end of his life, with the exception of two years, he lived, as far as his official duties permitted, for six months of every year. He worked at the *Analysis* during several successive vacations up to the year 1829 when it was published, and allowed me to read the manuscript portion by portion as it advanced. The other principal English writers on mental philosophy I read as I felt inclined, particularly Berkeley, Hume's *Essays,*[48] Reid, Dugald Stewart and Brown on *Cause and Effect.* Brown's *Lectures* I did not read

[47] First published in 1829; in 1869 an edition was published which was edited and annotated by J. S. Mill, with further notes by Alexander Bain, Andrew Findlater, and George Grote.—F. W. G.

[48] David Hume's *Essays Moral and Political* was published in 1741/42; Mill may be intending a reference to the *Enquiries* (see p. 146).—F. W. G.

until two or three years later, nor at that time had my father himself read them.

Among the works read in the course of this year which contributed materially to my development I ought to mention a book (written on the foundation of some of Bentham's manuscripts and published under the pseudonym of Philip Beauchamp) entitled *Analysis of the Influence of Natural Religion on the Temporal Happiness of Mankind.* This was an examination not of the truth but of the usefulness of religious belief in the most general sense apart from the peculiarities of any special revelation; which, of all the parts of the discussion concerning religion, is the most important in this age in which real belief in any religious doctrine is feeble and precarious, but the opinion of its necessity for moral and social purposes almost universal; and when those who reject revelation very generally take refuge in an optimistic deism, a worship of the order of Nature and the supposed course of Providence at least as full of contradictions and perverting to the moral sentiments as any of the forms of Christianity, if only it is as completely realised. Yet very little with any claim to a philosophical character has been written by sceptics against the usefulness of this form of belief. The volume bearing the name of Philip Beauchamp had this for its special object. Having been shown to my father in manuscript it was put into my hands by him, and I made a marginal analysis of it as I had done of the *Elements of Political Economy.* Next to the *Traités de Législation* it was one of the books which by the searching character of its analysis produced the greatest effect upon me. On reading it lately after an interval of many years I find it to have some of the defects as well as the merits of the Benthamic modes of thought and to contain, as I now think, many weak arguments, but with a great overbalance of sound ones and much good material for a more completely philosophic and conclusive treatment of the subject.

I have now, I believe, mentioned all the books which had any considerable effect on my early mental development. From this point I began to carry on my intellectual cultivation by writing still more than by reading.

Mill now describes his early ventures in writing, still under his father's guidance, and his association with his father's friends, George Grote and John and Charles Austin, to all of whom he was much indebted in the later stages of his education. He also describes the founding of the Utilitarian Society and the origin of its name: "I did not invent the word, but found it in one of Galt's novels, The Annals of the Parish, *in which the Scotch clergyman, of whom the book is a supposed autobiography, is represented as warning his parishioners not to leave the Gospel and become utilitarians." (The novel was published in 1821, but Jeremy Bentham had already used the word of himself in a letter to Dumont in 1802—see Packe's* Life of John Stuart Mill, *p. 53 n.; Mill is incorrect, therefore, in saying as he does here that "it was the first time anyone had taken the title of Utilitarian.")*

In May, 1823, my professional occupation and status for the next thirty-five years of my life were decided by my father's obtaining for me an appointment from the East India Company, in the office of the Examiner of India Correspondence, immediately under himself. I was appointed in the usual manner, at the bottom of the list of clerks, to rise, at least in the first instance, by seniority; but with the understanding that I should be employed from the beginning in preparing drafts of despatches, and be thus trained up as a successor to those who then filled the higher departments of the office. My drafts of course required for some time much revision from my immediate superiors, but I soon became well acquainted with the business, and by my father's instructions and the general growth of my own powers I was in a few years qualified to be, and practically was, the chief conductor of the correspondence with India in one of the leading departments, that of the Native States. This continued to be my official duty until I was appointed Examiner, only two years before the time when the abolition of the East India Company as a political body determined my retirement.[49] I do not know any one of the occupations by which a subsistence can now be gained more suitable than such as this to anyone who, not being in independent circumstances, desires to devote a part of the twenty-four hours to private intellectual pursuits. Writing for the press cannot be recommended as a permanent resource to anyone qualified to accomplish anything in the higher departments of literature or thought; not only on account of the uncertainty of this means of livelihood, especially if the writer has a conscience and will not consent to serve any opinions except his own, but also because the writings by which one can live are not the writings which themselves live and are never those in which the writer does his best. Books destined to form future thinkers take too much time to write, and when written come, in general, too slowly into notice and repute to be relied on for subsistence. Those who have to support themselves by their pen must depend on literary drudgery or at best on writings addressed to

[49] The East India Company ceded its powers to the British Government in 1858.—F. W. G.

the multitude, and can employ in the pursuits of their own choice only such time as they can spare from those of necessity (which is generally less than the leisure allowed by office occupations, while the effect on the mind is far more enervating and fatiguing). For my own part I have through life found office duties an actual rest from the other mental occupations which I have carried on simultaneously with them. They were sufficiently intellectual not to be a distasteful drudgery, without being such as to cause any strain upon the mental powers of a person used to abstract thought or to the labour of careful literary composition. The drawbacks (for every mode of life has its drawbacks) were not, however, unfelt by me. I cared little for the loss of the chances of riches and honours held out by some of the professions, particularly the bar, which had been, as I have already said, the profession thought of for me. But I was not indifferent to exclusion from Parliament and public life; and I felt very sensibly the more immediate unpleasantness of confinement to London, the holiday allowed by India House practice not exceeding a month in the year, while my taste was strong for a country life and my sojourn in France had left behind it an ardent desire of travelling. But though these tastes could not be freely indulged, they were at no time entirely sacrificed. I passed most Sundays throughout the year in the country, taking long rural walks on that day even when residing in London. The month's holiday was for a few years passed at my father's house in the country; afterwards a part or the whole was spent in tours, chiefly pedestrian, with some one or more of the young men who were my chosen companions, and at a later period in longer journeys or excursions, alone or with other friends. France, Belgium and Rhenish Germany were within easy reach of the annual holiday; and two longer absences, one of three, the other of six months, under medical advice, added Switzerland, the Tyrol and Italy to my list. Fortunately, also, both these journeys occurred rather early, so as to give the benefit and charm of the remembrance to a large portion of life.

I am disposed to agree with what has been surmised by others, that the opportunity which my official position gave me of learning by personal observation the necessary conditions of the practical conduct of public affairs has been of considerable value to me as a theoretical reformer of the opinions and institutions of my time. Not, indeed, that public business transacted on paper, to take effect on the other side of the globe, was of itself calculated to give much practical knowledge of life. But the occupation accustomed me to see and hear the difficulties of every course and the means of obviating them stated and discussed deliberately with a view to execution; it gave me opportunities of perceiving when public measures and other political facts did not produce the effects which had been expected of them and from what causes; above all it was valuable to me by making me, in this portion of my activity, merely one wheel in a machine, the whole of which had to work together. As a speculative writer I should have had no one to consult but myself, and should have encountered in my speculations none of the obstacles which would have started up whenever they came to be applied to practice. But as a Secretary conducting political correspondence I could not issue an order or express an opinion without satisfying various persons very unlike myself that the thing was fit to be done. I was thus in a good position for finding out by practice the mode of putting a thought which gives it easiest admittance into minds not prepared for it by habit; while I became practically conversant with the difficulties of moving bodies of men, the necessities of compromise, the art of sacrificing the non-essential to preserve the essential. I learnt how to obtain the best I could when I could not obtain everything; instead of being indignant or dispirited because I could not have entirely my own way, to be pleased and encouraged when I could have the smallest part of it; and when even that could not be, to bear with complete equanimity the being overruled altogether. I have found, through life, these acquisitions to be of the greatest possible importance for personal happiness, and they are also a very necessary condition for enabling anyone, either as theorist or as practical man, to effect the greatest amount of good compatible with his opportunities.

IV

Youthful Propagandism. *The Westminster Review*

In the early part of Chapter IV Mill tells of his first published writings, chiefly letters and notices of books in The Traveller *and* The Morning Chronicle, *and of the founding by Bentham of* The Westminster Review *to expound, in opposition to* The Edinburgh Review, *the radical views he shared with the Mills and their circle. He goes on to describe his father's character and opinions and the nature of his influence on the group of men associated with him and referred to as "the Benthamite school in philosophy and politics"—a very much looser association, he explains, than the words suggest.*

In the passage that now follows, Mill first describes the views of this group, of which, "as one of the most active of its very small number," he had an intimate knowledge; he then gives a brief critique of the impact of Benthamism on himself, particularly with regard to the exaltation of reason above feeling.

But though none of us, probably, agreed in every respect with my father, his opinions, as I said before, were the principal element which gave its colour and character to the little group of young men who were the first propagators of what was afterwards called "Philosophic Radicalism." Their mode of thinking was not characterized by Benthamism in any sense which has relation to Bentham as a chief or guide, but rather by a combination of Bentham's point of view with that of the modern political economy and with the Hartleian metaphysics.[50] Malthus's population principle was quite as much a banner and point of union among us as any opinion specially belonging to Bentham.[51] This great doctrine, originally brought forward as an argument against the indefinite improvability of human affairs, we took up with ardent zeal in the contrary sense, as indicating the sole means of realising that improvability by securing full employment at high wages to the whole labouring population through a voluntary restriction of the increase of their numbers. The other leading characteristics of the creed, which we held in common with my father, may be stated as follows.

In politics an almost unbounded confidence in the efficacy of two things, representative government and complete freedom of discussion. So complete was my father's reliance on the influence of reason over the minds of mankind, whenever it is allowed to reach them, that he felt as if all would be gained if the whole population were taught to read, if all sorts of opinions were allowed to be addressed to them by word and in writing, and if by means of the suffrage they could nominate a legisla-

[50] Hartley's association psychology (see Introduction, pp. 19–21; also pp. 98 and 121–124) dispensed with the concept of the soul as an immaterial substance influencing and influenced by the body. —F. W. G.

[51] Thomas Malthus *(An Essay on the Principle of Population,* 1798) maintained that population growth always tends to outstrip production and, if unchecked, must result in human misery. Mill was much influenced by this doctrine and agreed with the need to restrict population in order to achieve an agreeable quality of life. (See Packe's *Life of John Stuart Mill,* pp. 301 ff.; also pp. 56 ff. on Mill's distribution of birth control pamphlets.)—F. W. G.

ture to give effect to the opinions they adopted. He thought that when the legislature no longer represented a class interest, it would aim at the general interest, honestly and with adequate wisdom, since the people would be sufficiently under the guidance of educated intelligence to make in general a good choice of persons to represent them, and having done so to leave to those whom they had chosen a liberal discretion. Accordingly aristocratic rule, the government of the Few in any of its shapes, being in his eyes the only thing which stood between mankind and an administration of their affairs by the best wisdom to be found among them, was the object of his sternest disapprobation, and a democratic suffrage the principal article of his political creed, not on the ground of liberty, Rights of Man, or any of the phrases, more or less significant, by which up to that time democracy had usually been defended, but as the most essential of "securities for good government." In this, too, he held fast only to what he deemed essentials; he was comparatively indifferent to monarchical or republican forms—far more so than Bentham, to whom a king, in the character of "corrupter-general", appeared necessarily very noxious. Next to aristocracy, an established church or corporation of priests, as being by position the great depravers of religion and interested in opposing the progress of the human mind, was the object of his greatest detestation; though he disliked no clergyman personally who did not deserve it and was on terms of sincere friendship with several. In ethics his moral feelings were energetic and rigid on all points which he deemed important to human well-being, while he was supremely indifferent in opinion (though his indifference did not show itself in personal conduct) to all those doctrines of the common morality which he thought had no foundation but in asceticism and priestcraft. He looked forward, for example, to a considerable increase in freedom in the relations between the sexes, though without pretending to define exactly what would be or ought to be the precise conditions of that freedom. This opinion was connected in him with no sensuality either of a theoretical or of a practical kind. He anticipated, on the contrary, as one of the beneficial effects of increased freedom, that the imagination would no longer dwell upon the physical relation and its adjuncts and swell this into one of the principal objects of life—a perversion of the imagination and feelings which he regarded as one of the deepest seated and most pervading evils in the human mind. In psychology his fundamental doctrine was the formation of all human character by circumstances, through the universal principle of association, and the consequent unlimited possibility of improving the moral and intellectual condition of mankind by education. Of all his doctrines none was more important than this or needs more to be insisted on; unfortunately there is none which is more contradictory to the prevailing tendencies of speculation both in his time and since.

These various opinions were seized on with youthful fanaticism by the little knot of young men of whom I was one; and we put into them a sectarian spirit from which, in intention at least, my father was wholly free. What we (or rather a phantom substituted in the place of us) were sometimes by a ridiculous exaggeration called by others, namely a "school", some of us for a time really hoped and aspired to be. The French *philosophes*[52] of the eighteenth century were the example we sought to imitate,

[52] The *philosophes* were men of science, thinkers, and men of letters who shared a belief in the efficacy of human reason and a desire to remove beliefs and institutions which impeded it.—F. W. G.

and we hoped to accomplish no less results. No one of the set went to so great excesses in this boyish ambition as I did; which might be shown by many particulars, were it not a useless waste of space and time.

All this, however, is properly only the outside of our existence, or at least the intellectual part alone, and no more than one side of that. In attempting to penetrate inward and give any indication of what we were as human beings, I must be understood as speaking only of myself, of whom alone I can speak from sufficient knowledge; and I do not believe that the picture would suit any of my companions without many and great modifications.

I conceive that the description so often given of a Benthamite as a mere reasoning machine, though extremely inapplicable to most of those who have been designated by that title, was during two or three years of my life not altogether untrue of me. It was perhaps as applicable to me as it can well be to anyone just entering into life, to whom the common objects of desire must in general have at least the attraction of novelty. There is nothing very extraordinary in this fact; no youth of the age I then was can be expected to be more than one thing, and this was the thing I happened to be. Ambition and desire of distinction I had in abundance; and zeal for what I thought the good of mankind was my strongest sentiment, mixing with and colouring all others. But my zeal was as yet little else, at that period of my life, than zeal for speculative opinions. It had not its root in genuine benevolence or sympathy with mankind, though these qualities held their due place in my ethical standard. Nor was it connected with any high enthusiasm for ideal nobleness. Yet of this feeling I was imaginatively very susceptible; but there was at that time an intermission of its natural aliment, poetical culture, while there was a superabundance of the discipline antagonistic to it, that of mere logic and analysis. Add to this that, as already mentioned, my father's teachings tended to the undervaluing of feeling. It was not that he was himself cold-hearted or insensible; I believe it was rather from the contrary quality: he thought that feeling could take care of itself, that there was sure to be enough of it if actions were properly cared about. Offended by the frequency with which, in ethical and philosophical controversy, feeling is made the ultimate reason and justification of conduct, instead of being itself called on for a justification, while in practice actions the effect of which on human happiness is mischievous are defended as being required by feeling, and the character of a person of feeling obtains a credit for desert which he thought only due to actions, he had a real impatience of attributing praise to feeling or of any but the most sparing reference to it, either in the estimation of persons or in the discussion of things. In addition to the influence which this characteristic in him had on me and others, we found all the opinions to which we attached most importance constantly attacked on the ground of feeling. Utility was denounced as cold calculation; political economy as hard-hearted; anti-population doctrines as repulsive to the natural feelings of mankind. We retorted by the word "sentimentality", which, along with "declamation" and "vague generalities", served us as common terms of opprobrium. Although we were generally in the right, as against those who were opposed to us, the effect was that the cultivation of feeling (except the feelings of public and private duty) was not in much esteem among us and had very little place in the thoughts of most of us, myself in particular. What we principally thought of was to alter people's opinions, to make them believe according to evidence and know what was their real interest, which when they once knew, they would, we thought, by the instrument of opinion enforce a regard to it upon one another. While fully recognising the superior excellence of unselfish benevolence and love of justice, we did not expect the regeneration of mankind from any direct action on those sentiments, but from the effect of educated intellect enlightening the selfish feelings. Although this last is prodigiously important as a means of improvement in the hands of those who are themselves impelled by nobler principles of action, I do not believe that any one of the survivors of the Benthamites or Utilitarians of that day now relies mainly upon it for the general amendment of human conduct.

From this neglect both in theory and in practice of the cultivation of feeling naturally resulted, among other things, an undervaluing of poetry, and of imagination generally, as an element of human nature. It is, or was, part of the popular notion of Benthamites that they are enemies of poetry; this was partly true of Bentham himself; he used to say that "all poetry is misrepresentation", but in the sense in which he said it the same might have been said of all impressive speech, of all representation or inculcation more oratorical in its character than a sum in arithmetic. An article of Bingham's in the first number of the *Westminster Review*,[53] in which he offered as an explanation of something which he disliked in Moore that "Mr. Moore *is* a poet, and therefore is *not* a rea-

[53] *The Westminster Review* was first published in 1824 with the financial support of Jeremy Bentham; it was used by the Mills and their associates to spread their views on social and political reform. It was merged with *The London Review* in 1836 and thenceforth appeared as *The London and Westminster Review*. Peregrine Bingham (the younger) was a legal writer and reporter and a principal contributor to *The Westminster*.—F. W. G.

soner,"[54] did a good deal to attach the notion of hating poetry to the writers in the *Review*. But the truth was that many of us were great readers of poetry; Bingham himself had been a writer of it, while as regards me (and the same thing might be said of my father) the correct statement would be, not that I disliked poetry, but that I was theoretically indifferent to it. I disliked any sentiments in poetry which I should have disliked in prose; and that included a great deal. And I was wholly blind to its place in human culture as a means of educating the feelings. But I was always personally very susceptible to some kinds of it. In the most sectarian period of my Benthamism I happened to look into Pope's *Essay on Man*, and though every opinion in it was contrary to mine, I well remember how powerfully it acted on my imagination. Perhaps at that time poetical composition of any higher type than eloquent discussion in verse might not have produced a similar effect on me; at all events I seldom gave it an opportunity. This, however, was a mere passive state. Long before I had enlarged in any considerable degree the basis of my intellectual creed, I had obtained in the natural course of my mental progress poetic culture of the most valuable kind by means of reverential admiration for the lives and characters of heroic persons, especially the heroes of philosophy. The same inspiring effect which so many of the benefactors of mankind have left on record that they had experienced from Plutarch's *Lives* was produced on me by Plato's pictures of Socrates and by some modern biographies, above all by Condorcet's *Life of Turgot*, a book well calculated to rouse the best sort of enthusiasm, since it contains one of the wisest and noblest of lives delineated by one of the

[54] On Moore see p. 221, note, below.—F. W. G.

wisest and noblest of men. The heroic virtue of these glorious representatives of the opinions with which I sympathised deeply affected me, and I perpetually recurred to them, as others do to a favourite poet, when needing to be carried up into the more elevated regions of feeling and thought. I may observe, by the way, that this book cured me of my sectarian follies. The two or three pages beginning, "Il regardait toute secte comme nuisible,"[55] and explaining why Turgot always kept himself perfectly distinct from the Encyclopedists, sank deeply into my mind. I left off designating myself and others as Utilitarians, and by the pronoun "we" or any other collective designation I ceased to *afficher*[56] sectarianism. My real inward sectarianism I did not get rid of till later and much more gradually.

There follows an account of Mill's editing of Bentham's manuscript papers for the Rationale of Judicial Evidence *(published in five volumes in 1827) and of the consequent improvement in Mill's literary style. At this time, he tells us, he was also contributing to a new journal,* Parliamentary History and Review, *which published parliamentary debates set out according to subject and with comment by various writers (it survived for only three annual editions).*

While thus engaged in writing for the public, I did not neglect other modes of self-cultivation. It was at this time that I learnt German, beginning it on the Hamiltonian method,[57] for which purpose I and several of my

[55] "He regarded every sect as harmful."—F. W. G.

[56] "Parade," "advertise."—F. W. G.

[57] James Hamilton (1769–1829), English teacher and proponent of a method of teaching languages which discarded grammar and

companions formed a class. For several years from this period our social studies assumed a shape which contributed very much to my mental progress. The idea occurred to us of carrying on by reading and conversation a joint study of several of the branches of science which we wished to be masters of. We assembled to the number of a dozen or more. Mr. Grote[58] lent a room of his house in Threadneedle Street for the purpose, and his partner, Prescott, one of the three original members of the Utilitarian Society, made one among us. We met two mornings in every week from half-past eight till ten, at which hour most of us were called off to our daily occupations. Our first subject was political economy. We chose some systematic treatise as our textbook, my father's *Elements* being our first choice. One of us read aloud a chapter or some smaller portion of the book. The discussion was then opened and anyone who had an objection or other remark to make made it. Our rule was to discuss thoroughly every point raised, whether great or small, prolonging the discussion until all who took part were satisfied with the conclusion they had individually arrived at, and to follow up every topic of collateral speculation which the chapter or the conversation suggested, never leaving it until we had untied every knot which we found. We repeatedly kept up the discussion of some one point for several weeks, thinking in-

---

relied on literal word-for-word translation below each line of the original. A similar method had been suggested a century earlier by John Locke and incorporated in his edition of *Aesop's Fables* (1703).—F. W. G.

[58] On Grote see under Beauchamp, p. 141. For many years Grote worked in his father's bank in Threadneedle Street and after his marriage lived next door to it. The Utilitarian Society was founded by J. S. Mill in 1822; it met in a room of Bentham's house in London.—F. W. G.

tently on it during the intervals of our meetings, and contriving solutions of the new difficulties which had risen up in the last morning's discussion. When we had finished in this way my father's *Elements,* we went in the same way through Ricardo's *Principles of Political Economy* and Bailey's *Dissertation on Value.* These close and vigorous discussions were not only improving in a high degree to those who took part in them but brought out new views of some topics of abstract political economy. The theory of international values which I afterwards published emanated from these conversations, as did also the modified form of Ricardo's theory of profits laid down in my essay on profits and interest.[59] Those among us with whom new speculations chiefly originated were Ellis, Graham and I, though others gave valuable aid to the discussions, especially Prescott and Roebuck, the one by his knowledge, the other by his dialectical acuteness.[60] The theories of international values and of profits were excogitated and worked out in about equal proportions by myself and Graham; and if our original project had been executed, my *Essays on Some Unsettled Questions of Political Economy* would have been brought out along with some papers of his under our joint names. But when my exposition came to be written, I found that I had so much over-estimated my agreement with him, and he dissented so much from the most original of

[59] Mill refers here to his *Essays on Some Unsettled Questions of Political Economy,* which he names below.—F. W. G.

[60] William Ellis was an insurance underwriter by profession but found time to write numerous books on economic and social matters; he had a special interest in schools and founded a number of them, naming them after George Birkbeck, founder of the Mechanics Institutes. J. A. Roebuck was a close friend of Mill until he presumed to advise him on his relationship with Harriet Taylor. He was a Member of Parliament for many years and was made a Privy Councillor in 1878.—F. W. G.

the two essays, that on international values, that I was obliged to consider the theory as now exclusively mine, and it came out as such when published many years later. I may mention that among the alterations which my father made in revising his *Elements* for the third edition several were founded on criticisms elicited by these conversations; and in particular he modified his opinions (though not to the extent of our new speculations) on both the points to which I have adverted.

When we had enough of political economy, we took up the syllogistic logic in the same manner, Grote now joining us. Our first textbook was Aldrich, but being disgusted with its superficiality we reprinted one of the most finished among the many manuals of the school logic which my father, a great collector of such books, possessed, the *Manuductio ad Logicam* of the Jesuit, Du Trieu. After finishing this we took up Whateley's *Logic,* then first republished from the *Encyclopaedia Metropolitana,*[61] and finally the *Computatio sive Logica* of Hobbes. These books, dealt with in our manner, afforded a wide range for original metaphysical speculation; and most of what has been done in the first book of my *System of Logic*[62] to rationalise and correct the principles and distinctions of the school logicians and to improve the theory of the import of propositions had its origin in these discussions, Graham and I originating most of the novelties, while Grote and others furnished an excellent tribunal or test. From this time I formed the project of writing a book on logic, though on a much humbler scale than the one I ultimately executed.

Having done with logic we launched into analytic

[61] The *Encyclopaedia Metropolitana* was published in 25 volumes between 1817 and 1845.—F. W. G.

[62] Published 1843.—F. W. G.

psychology, and having chosen Hartley for our textbook, we raised Priestley's edition to an extravagant price by searching through London to furnish each of us with a copy.[63] When we had finished Hartley, we suspended our meetings; but my father's *Analysis of the Mind* being published soon after, we reassembled for the purpose of reading it. With this our exercises ended. I have always dated from these conversations my own real inauguration as an original and independent thinker. It was also through them that I acquired, or very much strengthened, a mental habit to which I attribute all that I have ever done or ever shall do in speculation—that of never accepting half-solutions of difficulties as complete; never abandoning a puzzle, but again and again returning to it until it was cleared up; never allowing obscure corners of a subject to remain unexplored because they did not appear important; never thinking that I perfectly understood any part of a subject until I understood the whole.

The rest of the chapter describes the founding, in 1825, and the early fortunes of the London Debating Society; see p. 124 and note 67, below.

[63] Joseph Priestley, *Hartley's Theory of the Human Mind, etc.* (1775).—F. W. G.

V

A Crisis in My Mental History. One Stage Onward

For some years after this time I wrote very little, and nothing regularly, for publication; and great were the advantages which I derived from the intermission. It was of no common importance to me at this period to be able to digest and mature my thoughts for my own mind only, without any immediate call for giving them out in print. Had I gone on writing, it would have much disturbed the important transformation in my opinions and character, which took place during those years. The origin of this transformation, or at least the process by which I was prepared for it, can only be explained by turning some distance back.

From the winter of 1821, when I first read Bentham, and especially from the commencement of the *Westminster Review,* I had what might truly be called an object in life—to be a reformer of the world. My conception of my own happiness was entirely identified with this object. The personal sympathies I wished for were those of fellow labourers in this enterprise. I endeavoured to pick up as many flowers as I could by the way; but as a serious and permanent personal satisfaction to rest upon, my whole reliance was placed on this, and I was accustomed to felicitate myself on the certainty of a happy life which I enjoyed through placing my happiness in something durable and distant, in which some progress might be always making, while it could never be exhausted by complete attainment. This did very well for several years, during which the general improvement going on in the world and the idea of myself as engaged with others in struggling to promote it seemed enough to fill up an interesting and animated existence. But the time came when I was awakened from this as from a dream. It was in the autumn of 1826. I was in a dull state of nerves, such as everybody is occasionally liable to, unsusceptible to enjoyment or pleasurable excitement; one of those moods when what is pleasure at other times becomes insipid or indifferent—the state, I should think, in which converts to Methodism usually are when smitten by their first "conviction of sin."[64] In this frame of mind it occurred to me to put the question directly to myself: "Suppose that all your objects in life were realised, that all the changes in institutions and opinions which you are looking forward to could be completely effected at this very instant, would this be a great joy and happiness to you?" And an irrepressible self-consciousness distinctly answered, "No!" At this my heart sank within me; the whole foundation on which my life was constructed fell down. All my happiness was to have been found in the continual pursuit of this end. The end had ceased to charm, and how could there ever again be any interest in the means? I seemed to have nothing left to live for.

At first I hoped that the cloud would pass away of itself; but it did not. A night's sleep, the sovereign remedy for the smaller vexations of life, had no effect on

[64] Such feelings are surely not confined to Methodists!—F. W. G.

it. I awoke to a renewed consciousness of the woeful fact. I carried it with me into all companies, into all occupations. Hardly anything had power to cause me even a few minutes' oblivion of it. For some months the cloud seemed to grow thicker and thicker. The lines in Coleridge's "Dejection"—I was not then acquainted with them—exactly describe my case:

> A grief without a pang, void, dark and drear,
> A drowsy, stifled, unimpassioned grief,
> Which finds no natural outlet or relief
> In word, or sigh, or tear.[65]

In vain I sought relief from my favourite books; those memorials of past nobleness and greatness from which I had always hitherto drawn strength and animation. I read them now without feeling, or with the accustomed feeling *minus* all its charm, and I became persuaded that my love of mankind and of excellence for its own sake had worn itself out. I sought no comfort by speaking to others of what I felt. If I had loved anyone sufficiently to make confiding my griefs a necessity, I should not have been in the condition I was. I felt, too, that mine was not an interesting or in any way respectable distress. There was nothing in it to attract sympathy. Advice, if I had known where to seek it, would have been most precious. The words of Macbeth to the physician often occurred to my thoughts.[66] But there was no one on whom I could build the faintest hope of such assistance.

[65] The lines are not quite correctly quoted:
"A stifled, drowsy unimpassioned grief,
Which finds no natural outlet, no relief. . . ."
—F. W. G.

[66] *Macbeth,* Act V, Scene iii:
"Canst thou not minister to a mind diseas'd?"
—F. W. G.

My father, to whom it would have been natural to me to have recourse in any practical difficulties, was the last person to whom, in such a case as this, I looked for help. Everything convinced me that he had no knowledge of any such mental state as I was suffering from, and that even if he could be made to understand it, he was not the physician who could heal it. My education, which was wholly his work, had been conducted without any regard to the possibility of its ending in this result; and I saw no use in giving him the pain of thinking that his plans had failed, when the failure was probably irremediable and, at all events, beyond the power of *his* remedies. Of other friends I had at that time none to whom I had any hope of making my condition intelligible. It was, however, abundantly intelligible to myself; and the more I dwelt upon it, the more hopeless it appeared.

My course of study had led me to believe that all mental and moral feelings and qualities, whether of a good or of a bad kind, were the results of association; that we love one thing and hate another, take pleasure in one sort of action or contemplation and pain in another sort, through the clinging of pleasurable or painful ideas to those things from the effect of education or of experience. As a corollary from this, I had always heard it maintained by my father, and was myself convinced, that the object of education should be to form the strongest possible associations of the salutary class, associations of pleasure with all things beneficial to the great whole and of pain with all things hurtful to it. This doctrine appeared inexpugnable; but it now seemed to me on retrospect that my teachers had occupied themselves but superficially with the means of forming and keeping up these salutary associations. They seemed to have trusted altogether to the old familiar instruments, praise and blame, reward and punishment. Now I did not doubt that by these means, begun early and applied unremittingly, intense associations of pain and pleasure, especially of pain, might be created, and might produce desires and aversions capable of lasting undiminished to the end of life. But there must always be something artificial and casual in associations thus produced. The pleasures and pains thus forcibly associated with things are not connected with them by any natural tie; and it is therefore, I thought, essential to the durability of these associations that they should have become so intense and inveterate as to be practically indissoluble before the habitual exercise of the power of analysis had commenced. For I now saw, or thought I saw, what I had always before received with incredulity, that the habit of analysis has a tendency to wear away the feelings—as indeed it has, when no other mental habit is cultivated and the analysing spirit remains without its natural complements and correctives. The very excellence of analysis (I argued) is that it tends to weaken and undermine whatever is the result of prejudice, that it enables us mentally to separate ideas which have only casually clung together; and no associations whatever could ultimately resist this dissolving force, were it not that we owe to analysis our clearest knowledge of the permanent sequences in nature, the real connections between things not dependent on our will and feelings, natural laws by virtue of which in many cases one thing is inseparable from another in fact; which laws, in proportion as they are clearly perceived and imaginatively realised, cause our ideas of things which are always joined together in nature to cohere more and more closely in our thoughts. Analytic habits may thus even strengthen the associations between causes and effects, means and ends, but tend altogether to weaken those which are, to speak familiarly, a *mere* matter of feeling. They are therefore (I thought) favourable to prudence and clearsightedness, but a perpetual worm at the root both of the passions and of the virtues; and, above all, fearfully undermine all desires and all pleasures which are the effects of association, that is, according to the theory I held, all except the purely physical and organic, of the entire insufficiency of which to make life desirable no one had a stronger conviction than I had. These were the laws of human nature, by which, as it seemed to me, I had been brought to my present state. All those to whom I looked up were of opinion that the pleasure of sympathy with human beings and the feelings which made the good of others, and especially of mankind on a large scale, the object of existence were the greatest and surest sources of happiness. Of the truth of this I was convinced, but to know that a feeling would make me happy if I had it did not give me the feeling. My education, I thought, had failed to create these feelings in sufficient strength to resist the dissolving influence of analysis, while the whole course of my intellectual cultivation had made precocious and premature analysis the inveterate habit of my mind. I was thus, as I said to myself, left stranded at the commencement of my voyage with a well-equipped ship and a rudder, but no sail, without any real desire for the ends which I had been so carefully fitted out to work for, no delight in virtue or the general good but also just as little in anything else. The fountains of vanity and ambition seemed to have dried up within me as completely as those of benevolence. I had had (as I reflected) some gratification of vanity at too early an age; I had obtained some distinction and felt myself of some importance before the desire of distinction and of importance had grown into a passion; and little as it was which I had attained, yet having been attained too early, like all pleasures enjoyed too soon, it had made me *blasé* and indifferent to the pursuit. Thus neither selfish nor unselfish pleasures were pleasures to me. And there seemed no power in nature sufficient to begin the formation of my character anew and create in a mind now irretrievably analytic fresh associations of pleasure with any of the objects of human desire.

These were the thoughts which mingled with the dry, heavy dejection of the melancholy winter of 1826-7. During this time I was not incapable of my usual occupations. I went on with them mechanically, by the mere force of habit. I had been so drilled in a certain sort of mental exercise, that I could still carry it on when all the spirit had gone out of it. I even composed and spoke several speeches at the debating society,[67] how, or with what degree of success, I know not. Of four years continual speaking at that society this is the only year of which I remember next to nothing. Two lines of Coleridge, in whom alone of all writers I have found a true description of what I felt, were often in my thoughts, not at this time (for I had never read them), but in a later period of the same mental malady:

> Work without hope draws nectar in a sieve,
> And hope without an object cannot live.[68]

In all probability my case was by no means so peculiar as I fancied it, and I doubt not that many others have

[67] The London Debating Society, founded 1825, at which Mill was a regular speaker.—F. W. G.

[68] From *Work without Hope: lines composed 21 February, 1827.* —F. W. G.

passed through a similar mental state; but the idiosyncrasies of my education had given to the general phenomenon a special character, which made it seem the natural effect of causes that it was hardly possible for time to remove. I frequently asked myself if I could or if I was bound to go on living, when life must be passed in this manner. I generally answered to myself that I did not think I could possibly bear it beyond a year. When, however, not more than half that duration of time had elapsed, a small ray of hope broke in upon my gloom. I was reading, accidentally, Marmontel's *Mémoires* and came to the passage which relates his father's death, the distressed position of the family and the sudden inspiration by which he, then a mere boy, felt and made them feel that he would be everything to them—would supply the place of all that they had lost.[69] A

[69] Jean François Marmontel (1723–1799), French man of letters; *Mémoires d'un père à ses enfants* (1804). After describing how he heard at College of his father's death, and his dismal journey home, Marmontel continues: "J'arrive, au milieu de la nuit, à la porte de ma maison. Je frappe, je me nomme, et, dans le moment, un murmure plaintif, un mélange de voix gémissantes se fait entendre. Toute la famille se lève, on vient m'ouvrir; et, en entrant, je suis environné de cette famille éplorée; mère, enfants, vieilles femmes, tous presque nus, échevelés, semblables à des spectres, et me tendant les bras avec des cris qui percent et déchirent mon cœur. Je ne sais quelle force que la nature nous réserve, sans doute, pour le malheur extrême, se déploya tout-à-coup en moi. J'avais à soulever un poids énorme de douleur; je n'y succombai point. J'ouvris mes bras, mon sein à cette foule de malheureux; je les y reçus tous; et, avec l'assurance d'un homme inspiré par le Ciel, sans marquer de faiblesse, sans verser une larme, moi qui pleure facilement: 'Ma mère, mes frères, mes sœurs, nous éprouvons, leur dis-je, la plus grande des afflictions; ne nous y laissons point abattre. Mes enfants, vous perdez un père; vous en retrouvez un, je vous en servirai; je le suis, je veux l'être; j'en embrasse tous les devoirs; et vous n'êtes plus orphelins.' A ces mots, des ruisseaux de larmes, mais des larmes bien moins amères, coulèrent de leurs yeux. 'Ah! s'écria ma mère, en me pressant contre son cœur, mon fils! mon cher enfant!

vivid conception of the scene and its feelings came over me, and I was moved to tears. From this moment my burden grew lighter. The oppression of the thought that all feeling was dead within me was gone. I was no longer hopeless; I was not a stock or a stone. I had still, it seemed, some of the material out of which all worth of character and all capacity for happiness are made. Relieved from my ever present sense of irremediable wretchedness, I gradually found that the ordinary incidents of life could again give me some pleasure; that I could again find enjoyment, not intense, but sufficient for cheerfulness, in sunshine and sky, in books, in conversation, in public affairs; and that there was, once more, excitement, though of a moderate kind, in exerting myself for my opinions and for the public good. Thus the cloud gradually drew off and I again enjoyed life; and though I had several relapses, some of which lasted many months, I never again was as miserable as I had been.

The experiences of this period had two very marked effects on my opinions and character. In the first place they led me to adopt a theory of life very unlike that on which I had before acted and having much in common with what at that time I certainly had never heard of, the anti-selfconsciousness theory of Carlyle.[70] I never, in-

---

que je t'ai bien connu.' Et mes frères, mes sœurs, mes bonnes tantes, ma grand'mère, tombèrent à genoux."—F. W. G.

[70] This is, briefly, that health, happiness, virtue, etc. are known, not in the possession of them, but in their absence. Carlyle was for a time a friend of J. S. Mill, though they were estranged in later years. Carlyle sent his partially complete manuscript of *The French Revolution* to Mill to read; by accident it found its way into Mill's wastepaper basket and was burnt. However, this was not the cause of the estrangement; Carlyle's response on this occasion was conspicuously generous.—F. W. G.

deed, wavered in the conviction that happiness is the test of all rules of conduct and the end of life. But I now thought that this end was only to be attained by not making it the direct end. Those only are happy (I thought) who have their minds fixed on some object other than their own happiness—on the happiness of others, on the improvement of mankind, even on some art or pursuit followed not as a means, but as itself an ideal end. Aiming thus at something else, they find happiness by the way. The enjoyments of life (such was now my theory) are sufficient to make it a pleasant thing, when they are taken *en passant* without being made a principal object. Once make them so, and they are immediately felt to be insufficient. They will not bear a scrutinising examination. Ask yourself whether you are happy, and you cease to be so. The only chance is to treat, not happiness, but some end external to it as the purpose of life. Let your self-consciousness, your scrutiny, your self-interrogation exhaust themselves on that; and, if otherwise fortunately circumstanced, you will inhale happiness with the air you breathe without dwelling on it or thinking about it, without either forestalling it in imagination or putting it to flight by fatal questioning. This theory now became the basis of my philosophy of life. And I still hold to it as the best theory for all those who have but a moderate degree of sensibility and of capacity for enjoyment, that is, for the great majority of mankind.

The other important change which my opinions at this time underwent was that I for the first time gave its proper place among the prime necessities of human well-being to the internal culture of the individual. I ceased to attach almost exclusive importance to the ordering of outward circumstances and the training of the human being for speculation and for action.

I had now learnt by experience that the passive susceptibilities needed to be cultivated as well as the active capacities, and required to be nourished and enriched as well as guided. I did not for an instant lose sight of or undervalue that part of the truth which I had seen before; I never turned recreant to intellectual culture or ceased to consider the power and practice of analysis as an essential condition both of individual and of social improvement. But I thought that it had consequences which required to be corrected by joining other kinds of cultivation with it. The maintenance of a due balance among the faculties now seemed to me of primary importance. The cultivation of the feelings became one of the cardinal points in my ethical and philosophical creed. And my thoughts and inclinations turned in an increasing degree towards whatever seemed capable of being instrumental to that object.

I now began to find meaning in the things which I had read or heard about the importance of poetry and art as instruments of human culture. But it was some time longer before I began to know this by personal experience. The only one of the imaginative arts in which I had from childhood taken great pleasure was music, the best effect of which (and in this it surpasses perhaps every other art) consists in exciting enthusiasm, in winding up to a high pitch those feelings of an elevated kind which are already in the character, but to which this excitement gives a glow and a fervour which, though transitory at its utmost height, is precious for sustaining them at other times. This effect of music I had often experienced; but like all my pleasurable susceptibilities it was suspended during the gloomy period. I had sought relief again and again from this quarter, but found none. After the tide had turned and I was in process of recovery, I had been helped forward by music, but in a much less elevated manner. I at this time first became acquainted with Weber's *Oberon,* and the extreme pleasure which I drew from its delicious melodies did me good by showing me a source of pleasure to which I was as susceptible as ever. The good, however, was much impaired by the thought that the pleasure of music (as is quite true of such pleasure as this was, that of mere tune) fades with familiarity and requires either to be revived by intermittence or fed by continual novelty. And it is very characteristic both of my then state and of the general tone of my mind at this period of my life, that I was seriously tormented by the thought of the exhaustibility of musical combinations. The octave consists only of five tones and two semitones, which can be put together in only a limited number of ways, of which but a small proportion are beautiful; most of these, it seemed to me, must have been already discovered and there could not be room for a long succession of Mozarts and Webers to strike out, as these had done, entirely new and surpassingly rich veins of musical beauty. This source of anxiety may, perhaps, be thought to resemble that of the philosophers of Laputa,[71] who feared lest the sun should be burnt out. It was, however, connected with the best feature in my character and the only good point to be found in my very unromantic and in no way honourable distress. For though my dejection, honestly looked at, could not be called other than egotistical, produced by the ruin, as I thought, of my fabric of happiness, yet the

[71] In Swift's *Gulliver's Travels,* Part III, Ch. 2.—F. W. G.

destiny of mankind in general was ever in my thoughts and could not be separated from my own. I felt that the flaw in my life must be a flaw in life itself; that the question was whether, if the reformers of society and government could succeed in their objects and every person in the community were free and in a state of physical comfort, the pleasures of life, being no longer kept up by struggle and privation, would cease to be pleasures. And I felt that unless I could see my way to some better hope than this for human happiness in general, my dejection must continue, but that if I could see such an outlet, I should then look on the world with pleasure, content, as far as I was myself concerned, with any fair share of the general lot.

This state of my thoughts and feelings made the fact of my reading Wordsworth for the first time (in the autumn of 1828) an important event in my life. I took up the collection of his poems from curiosity, with no expectation of mental relief from it, though I had before resorted to poetry with that hope. In the worst period of my depression I had read through the whole of Byron (then new to me) to try whether a poet whose peculiar department was supposed to be that of the intenser feelings could rouse any feeling in me. As might be expected, I got no good from this reading, but the reverse. The poet's state of mind was too like my own. His was the lament of a man who had worn out all pleasures and who seemed to think that life, to all who possess the good things of it, must necessarily be the vapid, uninteresting thing which I found it. His Harold and Manfred had the same burden on them which I had; and I was not in a frame of mind to desire any comfort from the vehement sensual passion of his Giaours or the sullenness of his Laras.[72] But while Byron was exactly what did not suit my condition, Wordsworth was exactly what did. I had looked into the *Excursion* two or three years before and found little in it; and I should probably have found as little, had I read it at this time. But the miscellaneous poems in the two-volume edition of 1815 (to which little of value was added in the latter part of the author's life) proved to be the precise thing for my mental wants at that particular juncture.

In the first place, these poems addressed themselves powerfully to one of the strongest of my pleasurable susceptibilities, the love of rural objects and natural scenery, to which I had been indebted, not only for much of the pleasure of my life, but quite recently for relief from one of my longest relapses into depression. In this power of rural beauty over me there was a foundation laid for taking pleasure in Wordsworth's poetry; the more so as his scenery lies mostly among mountains, which, owing to my early Pyrenean excursion, were my ideal of natural beauty. But Wordsworth would never have had any great effect on me, if he had merely placed before me beautiful pictures of natural scenery. Scott does this still better than Wordsworth, and a very second-rate landscape does it more effectually than any poet. What made Wordsworth's poems a medicine for my state of mind was that they expressed, not mere outward beauty, but states of feeling, and of thought coloured by feeling, under the excitement of beauty. They seemed to be the very culture of the feelings which I was in quest of. In them I seemed to draw from a source of inward joy, of sympathetic and

[72] The poems referred to are: *Childe Harold's Pilgrimage,* the dramatic poem *Manfred,* the *Giaour: a fragment of a Turkish Tale,* and *Lara.*—F. W. G.

imaginative pleasure, which could be shared in by all human beings, which had no connection with struggle or imperfection, but would be made richer by every improvement in the physical or social condition of mankind. From them I seemed to learn what would be the perennial sources of happiness, when all the greater evils of life shall have been removed. And I felt myself at once better and happier as I came under their influence. There have certainly been, even in our own age, greater poets than Wordsworth; but poetry of deeper and loftier feeling could not have done for me at that time what his did. I needed to be made to feel that there was real, permanent happiness in tranquil contemplation. Wordsworth taught me this, not only without turning away from, but with a greatly increased interest in, the common feelings and common destiny of human beings. And the delight which these poems gave me proved that with culture of this sort there was nothing to dread from the most confirmed habit of analysis. At the conclusion of the *Poems* came the famous Ode, falsely called Platonic,[73] "Intimations of Immortality", in which, along with more than his usual sweetness of melody and rhythm and along with the two passages of grand imagery but bad philosophy so often quoted, I found that he too had had similar experience to mine; that he also had felt that the first freshness of youthful enjoyment of life was not lasting; but that he had sought for compensation, and found it, in the way in which he was now teaching me to find it. The result was that I gradually, but completely, emerged from my habitual depression

[73] The line, "Our birth is but a sleep and a forgetting," suggests Plato's epistemological theory of "reminiscence," i.e., that the human soul acquires in a previous existence knowledge which is forgotten at birth and gradually recalled.—F. W. G.

and was never again subject to it. I long continued to value Wordsworth, less according to his intrinsic merits than by the measure of what he had done for me. Compared with the greatest poets he may be said to be the poet of unpoetical natures possessed of quiet and contemplative tastes. But unpoetical natures are precisely those which require poetic cultivation. This cultivation Wordsworth is much more fitted to give than poets who are intrinsically far more poets than he.

ADDITIONAL NOTES ON MILL'S READING

A. GREEK AUTHORS

AESCHINES (c. 389–314 B.C.): Athenian orator and opponent of Demosthenes (q.v.); he pursued a pro-Macedonian policy.

AESOP (early 6th century B.C.): his *Fables*—brief animal stories with a moral content—set the pattern for a type of literature which was enormously popular in the Middle Ages and after and was widely used in schools. Of later European fabulists the greatest is Jean de la Fontaine, whose *Fables Choisis* was published between 1668 and 1694. Joel Chandler Harris's *Uncle Remus* (1880) belongs to the same literary genus.

ANABASIS: see Xenophon.

ANACREON: Greek lyric poet, fl. 530 B.C.

ANTHOLOGY: the *Palatine Anthology* (so called because its manuscript was discovered in the library of the Elector Palatine at Heidelberg) is a compilation of Greek poetic epigrams taken, with considerable additions, from existing anthologies; it was put together by a Byzantine official, Cephalas, in the tenth century A.D.

ARISTOPHANES (c. 450–388 B.C.): greatest of the Athenian comic dramatists.

ARISTOTLE (384–322 B.C.): the Greek philosopher. The *Rhetoric* is concerned principally with the persuasiveness of arguments which are not logically cogent; in it Aristotle discusses oratory, forms of reasoning, appeals to emotion, and the types of emotion which the speakers may expect to excite; it is thus a work of considerable psychological interest, as Mill indicates (p. 49). His logical works are collectively known as the *Organon* ("tool," "instrument," i.e. of thought); Mill's logical studies began with this.

DEMOSTHENES (c. 383–322 B.C.): the greatest of the Greek orators. Of the thirty or forty speeches known to be authentic, nearly all are related to politics; the *Philippics*, for instance, is a series of speeches warning the Athenians against the growing power of Philip II of Macedon.

DIOGENES LAERTIUS (fl. 3rd century A.D.): his *Lives and Opinions of Famous Philosophers*, most of which is extant, is an important secondary source of information on the history of Greek philosophy.

DIONYSIUS (of Halicarnassus, a town in S.W. Asia Minor; fl. 30–10 B.C.): a rhetorician and historian who taught at Rome between 30 and 8 B.C.; apart from works of literary criticism, he wrote a history of Rome from its foundation to the first Punic War, *Antiquitates Romanae*.

EURIPIDES (c. 480–406 B.C.): the last of the great Athenian tragedians and perhaps, because of his psychological insight into human character and his controversial comment on contemporary life, the most modern; of his seventeen extant tragedies, *Medea*, *Alcestis*, and *Bacchae* are among the best known.

HERODOTUS (fl. 450 B.C.): the "father of history," the first European historian properly so called. In nine books named after the Muses he wrote an account of the wars between the Greeks and Persians; he is one of the liveliest and most readable of ancient authors.

ILIAD: see Pope, Alexander, p. 147.

ISOCRATES (435–338 B.C.): a teacher, pamphleteer, and writer of orations (for others to deliver). His stylistic theories were influential both in his own time and later among the Romans. The *Ad Demonicum* and *Ad Nicoclem* are both concerned with the duties of a monarch and contain moral and political precepts; Nicocles, the son of Evagoras, king of Salamis in Cyprus, was at one time a pupil of Isocrates.

LUCIAN (c. 125–190 A.D.): a Syrian by birth, he was noted for the excellence of his Greek style, his wit, and his satirical attacks on what he considered contemporary evils.

LYSIAS (fl. c. 412 B.C.): Athenian orator and writer of speeches; he was a skillful and polished writer, but not of the same caliber as Demosthenes.

ODYSSEY: see Pope, Alexander, p. 147.

PLATO (427–347 B.C.): Thrasyllus, a first-century A.D. scholar and editor, arranged Plato's dialogues in nine tetralogies or groups of four, which bear little or no relation to the chronological order of writing; this is the "common arrangement" to which Mill refers (p. 44); it is still to be found in the Oxford Text edition of Plato's works. The first six dialogues are: *Euthyphro, Apology, Crito, Phaedo, Cratylus, Theaetetus.* The last of these is concerned with difficult epistemological problems.

POLYBIUS (c. 203–120 B.C.): Greek historian of Rome with a high standard of historical truth; his work, which aimed to show how Rome established her supremacy over the Mediterranean world, covered the period from 266 to 120 B.C. in forty books; five complete books and large sections of eleven others are extant.

SOPHOCLES (c. 495–405 B.C.): Athenian tragedian whose best known plays include *Oedipus Rex* and *Antigone.*

THEOCRITUS (fl. 3rd century B.C.): a native of Syracuse; he is known chiefly for his *Idylls* (Greek, *eidyllion,* "a little sketch or scene") in which he depicts in dramatic form scenes mainly from country life. He is the first in a long line of pastoral poets, and Virgil (q.v.) and Milton are among his imitators.

THUCYDIDES (c. 460–399 B.C.): Athenian historian. His account of the Peloponnesian War between Athens and Sparta is one of the world's great historical works, remarkable for its impartiality and its critical analysis of military and political situations (see below, pp. 180–181 and note).

XENOPHON (c. 430–355 B.C.): the *Anabasis* describes the famous march (from Persia to the Black Sea, 401–400 B.C.) of ten thousand Greeks who had fought for Cyrus in his unsuccessful rebellion against his brother Artaxerxes, king of Persia. The *Cyropaedia* is a kind of moral romance, the earliest of its kind, describing the education and career of Cyrus the Great, founder of the Persian Empire. The *Memorabilia* (or *Memorials of Socrates,* as on p. 44) purports to be an account of Socratic conversations on various moral themes; it was intended as a defense of Socrates against his detractors. The *Hellenica,* a history of Greece, begins where Thucydides left off (411 B.C.) and continues to the death of the Theban Epaminondas in 362 B.C.; it is not a distinguished work.

B. ROMAN AUTHORS

CAESAR (Caius Julius Caesar, 101–44 B.C.): the *Commentaries (Commentarii de bello Gallico* and *de bello civili)* are his accounts of his campaigns in Gaul and Britain and of the civil war against the Pompeians.

CICERO (Marcus Tullius Cicero, 106–43 B.C.): most famous of the Roman orators and author of treatises on rhetoric and philosophy; he was also a great letter writer, and there are two major collections of his letters, one addressed to his intimate friend Atticus *(Ad Atticum)* and another to (and from) his wider circle of friends *(Ad familiares).* A French edition of the letters to Atticus was published by M. L. Mongault in 1714.

HORACE (Quintus Horatius Flaccus, 65–8 B.C.): best known for his lyric poetry, the four short books of the *Odes* (*carmina,* "songs," is the ancient title); the *Epodes* are also lyric poems, so called from the meter in which most of them are written. In addition Horace wrote (all in hexameters): the *Satires* (*saturae,* "miscellaneous pieces" —Horace calls them *sermones,* "familiar talks"); the *Epistles,* letters to friends on various themes; and the *Ars poetica,* a work of literary criticism which enjoyed enormous reputation and authority (not wholly deserved) in later centuries.

JUVENAL (Decimus Junius Juvenalis, c. 60–130 A.D.): the best known of Roman satirists and the last classical poet of importance.

LIVY (Titus Livius, 59–17 B.C.): his great history of Rome, *Ab urbe condita,* was written in 142 books, of which I–X and XXI–XLV are extant. The first ten books take the history of Rome from its foundation to the victory over the Samnites in 293 B.C.

LUCRETIUS (Titus Lucretius Carus, 94–55 B.C.): he wrote a didactic poem in six books, *De rerum natura,* expounding the Epicurean system of philosophy and attacking the conventional religion of his time; despite its purpose the poem has passages of great beauty.

NEPOS (Cornelius Nepos, c. 95–30 B.C.): his *Liber de excellentibus ducibus exterarum gentium* contains twenty-two short biographies of famous generals, all Greeks save for one Persian and the Carthaginians Hamilcar Barca and his son Hannibal.

OVID (Publius Ovidius Naso, 43 B.C.–18 A.D.): one of the best known, and within his genre, most skillful of Roman poets; his *Metamorphoses* is a collection of some 250 legends, all of which involve some sort of supernatural transformation; other works include *Amores,* an account of his amatory experiences, *Tristia,* written during his banishment to Tomi on the shores of the Black Sea, and the notorious *Ars amatoria,* a forerunner of modern sex manuals.

PHAEDRUS: a Thracian by birth, during the early years of the first century A.D. he wrote five books in verse of what he called *fabellae Aesopiae,* little stories after the fashion of Aesop. His work survives in extracts and for long was widely used as a Latin reader in the schools of Europe.

QUINTILIAN (Marcus Fabius Quintilianus, c. 30–96 A.D.): orator and teacher of rhetoric at Rome. His most important work is the *Institutio oratoria* ("The Education of an Orator") in twelve books; it is a primary source for Roman educational thought and practice in the first century and contains much educational wisdom.

SALLUST (Caius Sallustius Crispus, c. 86–35 B.C.): two works survive, monographs on the conspiracy of Catiline (63 B.C.) and the war against Jugurtha (108–105 B.C.); he is a vigorous writer with a style of his own.

TACITUS (Cornelius Tacitus, c. 55–120 A.D.): Roman historian; his extant works include *Agricola,* a brief biography of his father-in-law, who had been Roman governor of Britain; *Germania,* an account of the central European peoples; and *Historiae* and *Annales* (both incomplete), which together cover the events of most of the first century of the empire.

TERENCE (Publius Terentius Afer, c. 185–159 B.C.): next to Plautus the greatest writer of Latin comedy; six plays are extant, all of them based on Greek models, and their influence on European literature has been immense; until recent times they were widely used for school reading.

VIRGIL (Publius Virgilius Maro, 70–19 B.C.): *Bucolics* ("Pastoral Poems"), or *Eclogues* ("Select Poems"), are ten poems in the pastoral idiom; though written in terms of country themes and people, many of them carry political undertones. The *Aeneid,* his greatest work and one of the world's few great epic poems, is an account of the fall of Troy, the wanderings of Aeneas (legendary founder of the Roman nation), and the origins of Rome. The *Georgics,* a poem in four books of hexameter verse, is about farming and country life (p. 224 below).

C. LATER AUTHORS

ALDRICH, Henry (1647–1710): English ecclesiastic, author of *Artis Logicae Compendium* (1691), which was used as a textbook in logic for some two hundred years.

ANCIENT UNIVERSAL HISTORY: this seems to be *An Universal History from the earliest Account of Time to the Present,* published in sixty volumes between 1779 and 1784, of which the first eighteen were concerned with ancient history.

ANNUAL REGISTER: an annual record of events of the year in Great Britain and elsewhere, conceived originally by the poet and dramatist Robert Dodsley and first published in 1759; it is now published by Longmans, Green and Co. under the title *Annual Register of World Events.*

ANSON, George, first Baron (1697–1762): the English admiral famed for his exploits against the French and Spanish and for his circumnavigation of the world between 1740 and 1744.

ARABIAN NIGHTS: a collection of stories of uncertain date and authorship also known as *The Arabian Nights' Entertainment* and *The Thousand and One Nights* (1001 = a very large number); it includes such well-known stories as Aladdin, Ali Baba, and Sinbad the Sailor. The first European translation was by the French writer Antoine Galland, published between 1704 and 1717; of English translations the best known is perhaps Sir Richard Burton's *The Thousand Nights and a Night* (1885–1888).

BAILEY, Samuel (1791–1870): philosophical writer; *A Critical Dissertation on the Nature, Measures and Causes of Value* was published in 1825 and was directed against the account of value given by James Mill and Ricardo.

BAILLIE, Joanna (1762–1851): poet and dramatist. The play mentioned in Mill's note (p. 53) appeared in *Miscellaneous Plays,* published in 1804; its theme was taken from Gibbon's account of the siege of Constantinople by the Turks; it was produced with fair success in London and elsewhere.

BEATTIE: presumably James Beattie (1735–1803), poet and moral philosopher; his most celebrated poem, *The Minstrel* (1771), was a forerunner of the romantic revival.

BEAUCHAMP, Philip: pseudonym of George Grote (1794–1871), English historian and politician, who was a close friend of the Mills; he is best known for his *History of Greece,* which appeared in twelve volumes between 1846 and 1856; he also published *Plato and the Other Companions of Socrates* (3 vols., 1865), which was reviewed at great length by Mill in the *Edinburgh Review,* April 1866. The *Analysis* referred to on p. 99 was an edited and largely rewritten version of some papers of Bentham. (See also p. 114, note.)

BEAVER, Philip (1766–1813): a captain in the Royal Navy; he took part in an abortive attempt to colonize the island of Bulama, off the coast of Sierra Leone, and later wrote of his experiences in *African Memoranda* (1805).

BENTHAM, Jeremy: see the note, p. 46.

BERKELEY, George (1685–1753): bishop and philosopher, celebrated for his doctrine that *esse* is *percipi*, "to exist is to be perceived"; his principal works are *Essay towards a New Theory of Vision* (1709), *The Principles of Human Knowledge* (1710), and *Three Dialogues between Hylas and Philonous* (1713).

BLACKSTONE, Sir William (1723–1780): English jurist celebrated for his *Commentaries on the Laws of England* (4 vols., 1765–1769).

BROOKE, Henry (1703?–1783): Irish writer and friend of the poet Alexander Pope; his best known work is the novel, *The Fool of Quality; or the History of Henry, Earl of Moreland* (5 vols., 1766).

BROWN, Thomas (1778–1820): Scottish metaphysical philosopher; jointly with Dugald Stewart he held the Chair of Moral Philosophy at Edinburgh University. His essay, *Observations on the Nature and Tendency of the Doctrine of Mr. Hume concerning the relation of Cause and Effect* (1804), was intended to show that Hume's theories did not necessarily have the skeptical consequences ascribed to them and were not incompatible with Christianity.

BURNET, Gilbert (1643–1715): English bishop and historian, a member of the newly established Royal Society, and for a time professor of divinity at the University of Glasgow. A staunch Protestant, he fell foul of the Catholic James II of England, fled to Holland, and was there naturalized as a Dutch subject to avoid a possible prosecution for treason in England. At the revolution of

1688 he returned with William and Mary and wrote for them the text of their declaration. Apart from his *History of his Own Times* (1724–1734), he wrote a *History of the Reformation of the Church of England* (3 vols., 1679–1715).

CAMPBELL, Thomas (1777–1844): Scottish poet, one of the founders of University College, London, and from 1827 to 1829 Lord Rector of the University of Glasgow. The modern reader is unlikely to find in *Gertrude of Wyoming* (1809) the qualities that appealed to Mill.

CAZOTTE, Jacques: eighteenth-century French writer; the *Arabian Tales* was a continuation of *Arabian Nights* (q.v.); an English version of Cazotte's French translation from the Arabic was published in London in 1794.

CERVANTES, Saavedra, Miguel de (1547–1616): the famous Spanish novelist, playwright, and poet; *El Ingenioso Hidalgo Don Quixote de la Mancha* was published in Madrid in 1605 and was an immediate success; the first English version was Thomas Shelton's of 1612.

COLLINS, David (1756–1810): lieutenant colonel and colonial governor. In 1787 he sailed with an expedition to establish a convict settlement at Botany Bay, in New South Wales, Australia, which had recently been discovered by Captain Cook; a more suitable site was found at Port Jackson, where Sydney was later founded; after nine years he returned home and wrote *Judge Advocate of New South Wales: an Account of the English Colony in New South Wales . . . compiled from the MSS of Lieutenant-Governor King* (2 vols., 1798–1802).

CONDORCET, Marie Jean etc., Marquis de (1743–1794): French mathematician, philosopher, and reformer; his *Vie de M. Turgot* (French statesman and economist) was published in 1786.

COWPER, William (1731–1800): English poet and writer of hymns; his major poetical work, *The Task,* an account of rural life, was published in 1785, and a translation of Homer in 1791. See also p. 54 and note.

DON QUIXOTE: see Cervantes.

DRYDEN, John (1631–1700): English poet, dramatist, and critic; a major literary figure of the seventeenth century and a prolific writer. The ode *Alexander's Feast; or the Power of Musique* (1697) has been regarded by some—including Dryden himself!—as the height of achievement in English lyric poetry.

DU TRIEU: I have not been able to trace the *Manuductio ad Logicam,* mentioned on p. 116.

EDGEWORTH, Maria (1767–1849): Anglo-Irish novelist, best known for her children's stories and her portrayal of Irish life; she also wrote on educational reform. *Popular Tales* was published in 1804. See also p. 87 and note.

FERGUSON, Adam (1723–1816): professor of philosophy at the University of Edinburgh and a friend of David Hume, whom he succeeded as librarian of the Advocates Library in Edinburgh; the Roman history was published in 1783, entitled *The History of the Progress and Termination of the Roman Republic.*

GIBBON, Edward (1737–1794): English historian whose outstanding work is *The History of the Decline and Fall of the Roman Empire,* from the second century A.D. to the fall of Constantinople in 1453.

HARTLEY, David (1705–1757): English philosopher; he was the first to give systematic exposition, in his *Observations on Man* (1749), to the psychological doctrine of the association of ideas; an edition of this work was published by Joseph Priestley in 1775 under the title, *Hart-*

ley's Theory of the Human Mind. See p. 106 and note; also Introduction, pp. 19–20.

HAWKESWORTH, John (1715?–1773): author and editor; he was commissioned to revise and publish an account of recent voyages to the South Seas; the work appeared in three volumes in 1773 under the title *An Account of the Voyages undertaken by order of his present Majesty for making Discoveries in the Southern Hemisphere and successively performed by Commodore Byron, Captain Wallis, Captain Cartaret and Captain Cook, in the Dolphin, the Swallow and the Endeavour; drawn up from the journals which were kept by the several commanders and from the papers of Joseph Burks. . . .* A four-volume edition was published in Perth, Scotland, in 1789; nevertheless it seems likely that Mill was misremembering here, since with this title the book would hardly start with Drake (p. 47).

HELVETIUS, Claude Adrien (1715–1771): French philosopher of Swiss origin; his chief work, *De l'Esprit* (1758), was condemned by the Sorbonne and burned by the public hangman. Like Locke (q.v.) and Condillac (p. 92, note 39), he derived knowledge from sensation and drew the conclusion that all men are equal in cognitive potential and that, therefore, "l'éducation peut tout."

HOBBES, Thomas (1588–1679): English philosopher, best known now for his *Leviathan; or the Matter, Form and Power of a Commonwealth, Ecclesiastical and Civil* (1651); but he wrote numerous other works in English and Latin on politics, mathematics, science, and philosophy; he also translated Thucydides and Homer's *Iliad* and *Odyssey.* The *Computatio sive Logica* (p. 55) is the first part of a larger Latin work, *Elementorum Philosophiae Sectio Prima, de Corpore* (1655; English translation, 1656).

HOOKE, Nathaniel (d. 1763): his *Roman History from the*

Building of Rome to the Ruin of the Commonwealth was published in four volumes between 1738 and 1771; he was a friend of the poet Alexander Pope.

HUME, David (1711–1776): Scottish philosopher and historian. He belongs to the empirical tradition of philosophy, to which he contributed a strong skeptical element of his own. His principal philosophical works are *A Treatise of Human Nature* (1739–1740) and a revision and reshaping of this, *Enquiry concerning Human Understanding* (1748), and *Enquiry concerning the Principles of Morals* (1751). His *History of England* from Caesar's invasion to 1688 was published in six volumes between 1754 and 1762.

JOYCE, Jeremiah (1763–1816): editor and author of many popular works on scientific subjects; *Scientific Dialogues* was published in 1807 and often reprinted.

LANGHORNE, John (1735–1779): English poet; the translation of Plutarch's *Lives,* undertaken with his brother William, was published in 1770 and frequently reprinted.

LOCKE, John (1632–1704): English philosopher and "father of modern empiricism"; the *Essay concerning Human Understanding* was written over seventeen years and published in 1690.

MCCRIE, Thomas (1772–1835): Scottish ecclesiastical historian; his *Life of John Knox* (1811) is notable both for its erudition and its biographical skill.

MILLAR, John (1735–1801): professor of law at the University of Glasgow from 1761; the full title of the book which Mill names is *Historical View of the English Government from the Settlement of the Saxons in Britain to the Accession of the House of Stewart* (1787).

MITFORD, William (1744–1827): the first volume of the *History of Greece* was published in 1784, the second in

1790, but the book was not finished until 1810; though popular for many years, it was criticized adversely for its style, chronological errors, and political bias.

MOSHEIN, Johann Lorenz von (1693–1755): German Lutheran theologian, professor of divinity at Helmstedt and later at Gottingen, and a pioneer in the critical and objective treatment of original sources of ecclesiastical history. His *Institutiones historiae ecclesiasticae* (1726) was published in an English translation by A. Maclaine in 1765.

POPE, Alexander (1688–1744): the English poet; his translations of Homer's *Iliad* and *Odyssey* (the latter with the help of others) are perhaps his greatest achievement; they secured both his reputation and his financial position. Mill also mentions (p. 112) that he was greatly impressed by his *Essay on Man*.

REID, Thomas (1710–1796): Scottish philosopher who opposed his "philosophy of common sense" to the skeptical views of Hume; his philosophical works are *An Inquiry into the Human Mind on the Principles of Common Sense* (1764); *Essays on the Intellectual Powers of Man* (1785), and *Essays on the Active Powers of Man* (1788).

RICARDO, David (1772–1823): a pioneer in economic theory; his chief work is *Principles of Political Economy and Taxation* (1817). He also made an important contribution to the theory of banking in three pamphlets, *The High Price of Bullion, Proposals for an Economic and Secure Currency,* and *Plan for a National Bank.*

ROBERTSON, William (1721–1793): Scottish historian and Presbyterian minister; his writings, which were widely popular in his time, included a history of Scotland in the reigns of Queen Mary and James VI, an account of the reign of the Emperor Charles V of Spain, and a *History of America* (i.e. Spanish America).

ROLLIN, Charles (1661–1741): French historian and rector of the University of Paris; his *Histoire Ancienne* (13 vols., 1730–1738) was immensely popular at the time—an English translation reached its eighteenth edition in 1839.

RUTTY, John (1698–1775): himself a Quaker, he published in 1751 *A History of the Rise and Progress of the People called Quakers in Ireland from 1653 to 1751.*

SEWEL, William (1654–1720): son of an English Quaker who had fled to Holland to escape religious persecution; *The History of the Rise, Increase and Progress of the Christian People called Quakers,* which took him twenty-five years to prepare, was published in Dutch in 1717 and in an English translation in 1722.

SMITH, Adam (1723–1790): the founder of political economy as a distinct branch of knowledge, his chief contribution to this being his celebrated *Inquiry into the Nature and Causes of the Wealth of Nations* (1776).

STEWART, Dugald (1753–1828): Scottish philosopher and professor of moral philosophy at Edinburgh University from 1785; the first volume of *Elements of the Philosophy of the Human Mind* was published in 1792 and later volumes in 1814 and 1827; he also wrote on moral philosophy.

THOMSON, James (1700–1748): poet and playwright whose work was enormously popular during the century after his death; his poem *Winter* was published in 1726. His most famous (or infamous?) composition is the song "Rule Britannia."

THOMSON, Thomas (1773–1852): a distinguished chemist and a Fellow of the Royal Society, he was noted for his support of Dalton's atomic theory; he also established in Edinburgh what may have been the first chemistry laboratory in the United Kingdom for instructional purposes. His *System of Chemistry* was published in 1802;

the third edition of this (1807) contained the first detailed public announcement of Dalton's atomic theory (Dalton's *New System of Chemical Philosophy* was published in the following year). He was a contemporary of James Mill at Edinburgh University and remained a close friend.

WATSON, Robert (1730?–1781): his *History of Philip II of Spain* was published in two volumes in 1777; a very popular work, it reached a seventh edition by 1812 and was translated into French, German, and Dutch. His *History of the Reign of Philip III of Spain* was unfinished at the time of his death; it was completed by Dr. William Thomson and published in 1783.

WHATELEY, Richard (1787–1863): Fellow of Oriel College, Oxford, and later archbishop of Dublin. His *Elements of Logic* (1826) was originally published as an article contributed to the *Encyclopaedia Metropolitana;* it has serious deficiencies despite Mill's praise in his review in *The Westminster Review,* January 1828.

Inaugural Address
at the University of St. Andrews

A NOTE ON THE TEXT

The text which follows is that of the People's Edition, published in 1867 by Longmans, Green, Reader and Dyer. As in the *Autobiography,* I have made some minor alterations to punctuation and typography.

Inaugural Address at the University of St. Andrews

In complying with the custom which prescribes that the person whom you have called by your suffrages to the honorary presidency of your University should embody in an Address a few thoughts on the subjects which most nearly concern a seat of liberal education, let me begin by saying that this usage appears to me highly commendable. Education, in its larger sense, is one of the most inexhaustible of all topics. Though there is hardly any subject on which so much has been written by so many of the wisest men, it is as fresh to those who come to it with a fresh mind, a mind not hopelessly filled full with other people's conclusions, as it was to the first explorers of it; and notwithstanding the great mass of excellent things which have been said respecting it, no thoughtful person finds any lack of things both great and small still waiting to be said, or waiting to be developed and followed out to their consequences. Education, moreover, is one of the subjects which most essentially require to be considered by various minds and from a variety of points of view. For of all many-sided subjects it is the one which has the greatest number of sides. Not only does it include whatever we do for ourselves and whatever is done for us by others for the express purpose of bringing us somewhat nearer to the perfection of our nature; it does more: in its largest acceptation it comprehends even the indirect effects produced on character and on the human faculties by things of which the direct purposes are quite different; by laws, by forms of government, by the industrial arts, by modes of social life; nay, even by physical facts not dependent on human will, by climate, soil and local position. Whatever helps to shape the human being, to make the individual what he is or hinder him from being what he is not, is part of his education. And a very bad education it often is, requiring all that can be done by cultivated intelligence and will to counteract its tendencies. To take an obvious instance: the niggardliness of Nature in some places, by engrossing the whole energies of the human being in the mere preservation of life, and her over-bounty in others, affording a sort of brutish subsistence on too easy terms, with hardly any exertion of the human faculties, are both hostile to the spontaneous growth and development of the mind; and it is at those two extremes of the scale that we find human societies in the state of most unmitigated savagery. I shall confine myself, however, to education in the narrower sense—the culture which each generation purposely gives to those who are to be its successors in order to qualify them for at least keeping up, and if possible for raising, the level of improvement which has been attained. Nearly all here present are daily occupied either in receiving or in giving this sort of education; and the part of it which most concerns you at present is that in which you are yourselves engaged—the stage of education which is the appointed business of a national university.

The proper function of a university in national education is tolerably well understood.[1] At least there is a

[1] This is the particular theme of Discourse VII of J. H. Newman's *The Idea of a University,* first published in 1852 under the title, *Discourses on the Scope and Nature of University Education.*

tolerably general agreement about what a university is not. It is not a place of professional education. Universities are not intended to teach the knowledge required to fit men for some special mode of gaining their livelihood. Their object is not to make skilful lawyers or physicians or engineers, but capable and cultivated human beings. It is very right that there should be public facilities for the study of professions. It is well that there should be Schools of Law and of Medicine, and it would be well if there were schools of engineering and the industrial arts. The countries which have such institutions are greatly the better for them; and there is something to be said for having them in the same localities and under the same general superintendence as the establishments devoted to education properly so called. But these things are no part of what every generation owes to the next, as that on which its civilisation and worth will principally depend. They are needed only by a comparatively few, who are under the strongest private inducements to acquire them by their own efforts; and even those few do not require them until after their education, in the ordinary sense, has been completed. Whether those whose speciality they are will learn them as a branch of intelligence or as a mere trade, and whether, having learnt them, they will make a wise and conscientious use of them or the reverse depends less on the manner in which they are taught their profession than upon what sort of minds they bring to it—what kind of intelligence and of conscience the general system of education has de-

---

Newman attacks the "utility" concept of education, which restricts it to a narrow professional or scientific training, and pleads for the "cultivated intellect" which "because it is a good in itself, brings with it a power and a grace to every work and occupation which it undertakes." Newman, *The Idea of a University,* ed. C. F. Harrold (New York: Longmans, Green, 1947), p. 148.—F. W. G.

veloped in them. Men are men before they are lawyers or physicians or merchants or manufacturers; and if you make them capable and sensible men, they will make themselves capable and sensible lawyers or physicians. What professional men should carry away with them from a university is not professional knowledge, but that which should direct the use of their professional knowledge and bring the light of general culture to illuminate the technicalities of a special pursuit. Men may be competent lawyers without general education, but it depends on general education to make them philosophic lawyers —who demand, and are capable of apprehending, principles, instead of merely cramming their memory with details.[2] And so of all other useful pursuits, mechanical included. Education makes a man a more intelligent shoemaker, if that be his occupation, but not by teaching him how to make shoes; it does so by the mental exercise it gives and the habits it impresses.

This, then, is what a mathematician would call the higher limit of university education; its province ends where education, ceasing to be general, branches off into departments adapted to the individual's destination in life. The lower limit is more difficult to define. A university is not concerned with elementary instruction; the pupil is supposed to have acquired that before coming here. But where does elementary instruction end and the higher studies begin? Some have given a very wide extension to the idea of elementary instruction. According to them it is not the office of a university to give instruction in single branches of knowledge from the commencement. What the pupil should be taught here (they think) is to methodise his knowledge: to look at every separate

[2] Cf. *Autobiography*, p. 66 and note.—F. W. G.

part of it in its relation to the other parts and to the whole; combining the partial glimpses which he has obtained of the field of human knowledge at different points into a general map, if I may so speak, of the entire region; observing how all knowledge is connected, how we ascend to one branch by means of another, how the higher modifies the lower and the lower helps us to understand the higher; how every existing reality is a compound of many properties, of which each science or distinct mode of study reveals but a small part, but the whole of which must be included to enable us to know it truly as a fact in Nature and not as a mere abstraction.

This last stage of general education destined to give the pupil a comprehensive and connected view of the things which he has already learnt separately includes a philosophic study of the methods of the sciences, the modes in which the human intellect proceeds from the known to the unknown. We must be taught to generalise our conception of the resources which the human mind possesses for the exploration of nature; to understand how man discovers the real facts of the world and by what tests he can judge whether he has really found them. And doubtless this is the crown and consummation of a liberal education; but before we restrict a university to this highest department of instruction—before we confine it to teaching, not knowledge, but the philosophy of knowledge—we must be assured that the knowledge itself has been acquired elsewhere. Those who take this view of the function of a university are not wrong in thinking that the schools, as distinguished from the universities, ought to be adequate to teaching every branch of general instruction required by youth, so far as it can be studied apart from the rest. But where are such schools to be found? Since science assumed its modern character, nowhere; and in these islands[3] less even than elsewhere. This ancient kingdom,[4] thanks to its great religious reformers, had the inestimable advantage, denied to its southern sister, of excellent parish schools which gave, really and not in pretence, a considerable amount of valuable literary instruction to the bulk of the population two centuries earlier than in any other country. But schools of a still higher description have been, even in Scotland, so few and inadequate that the universities have had to perform largely the functions which ought to be performed by schools, receiving students at an early age and undertaking not only the work for which the schools should have prepared them, but much of the preparation itself. Every Scottish university is not a university only, but a high school, to supply the deficiency of other schools. And if the English universities do not do the same, it is not because the same need does not exist, but because it is disregarded. Youths come to the Scottish universities ignorant and are there taught. The majority of those who come to the English universities come still more ignorant, and ignorant they go away.[5]

In point of fact, therefore, the office of a Scottish university comprises the whole of a liberal education from the foundations upwards. And the scheme of your universities has, almost from the beginning, really aimed at including the whole, both in depth and in breadth. You

[3] The British Isles.—F. W. G.

[4] Scotland.—F. W. G.

[5] In *The London Review,* April 1835, Mill strongly attacks the English universities in his review (reprinted in *Dissertations and Discussions,* Vol. I) of Professor Sedgwick's *Discourse on the Studies of the University;* and again in his review of Dr. William Whewell's *Lectures on the History of Moral Philosophy in England* in *The Westminster Review,* October 1852 (reprinted in *Dissertations and Discussions,* Vol. II).—F. W. G.

have not, as the English universities so long did, confined all the stress of your teaching, all your real effort to teach, within the limits of two subjects, the classical languages and mathematics. You did not wait till the last few years to establish a Natural Science and a Moral Science Tripos.[6] Instruction in both those departments was organised long ago; and your teachers of those subjects have not been nominal professors who did not lecture; some of the greatest names in physical and in moral science have taught in your universities and by their teaching contributed to form some of the most distinguished intellects of the last and present centuries. To comment upon the course of education at the Scottish universities is to pass in review every essential department of general culture. The best use, then, which I am able to make of the present occasion is to offer a few remarks on each of those departments, considered in its relation to human cultivation at large: adverting to the nature of the claims which each has to a place in liberal education; in what special manner they each conduce to the improvement of the individual mind and the benefit of the race; and how they all conspire to the common end, the strengthening, exalting, purifying and beautifying of our common nature, and the fitting out of mankind with the necessary mental implements for the work they have to perform through life.

Let me first say a few words on the great controversy of the present day with regard to the higher education, the difference which most broadly divides educational reformers and conservatives: the vexed question between

[6] Triposes (degree courses) in Natural Sciences and in Moral Sciences were introduced at Cambridge about 1850; Oxford instituted a Final Honours School of Natural Science at much the same time—F. W. G.

the ancient languages and the modern sciences and arts; whether general education should be classical—let me use a wider expression and say literary—or scientific; a dispute as endlessly and often as fruitlessly agitated as that old controversy[7] which it resembles, made memorable by the names of Swift and Sir William Temple in England and Fontenelle in France—the contest for superiority between the ancients and the moderns. This question, whether we should be taught the classics or the sciences, seems to me, I confess, very like a dispute whether painters should cultivate drawing or colouring, or, to use a more homely illustration, whether a tailor should make coats or trousers. I can only reply by the question, Why not both? Can anything deserve the name of a good education which does not include literature and science too? If there were no more to be said than that scientific education teaches us to think and literary education to express our thoughts, do we not require both? And is not anyone a poor, maimed, lopsided fragment of humanity who is deficient in either? We are not obliged to ask ourselves whether it is more important to know the languages or the sciences. Short as life is, and shorter still as we make it by the time we waste on things which are neither business nor meditation nor pleasure, we are not so badly off that our scholars need be ignorant of the laws and properties of the world they live in or our scientific men destitute of poetic feeling and artistic cultivation. I am amazed at

[7] Mill refers to the argument which took place towards the end of the seventeenth century over the comparative merits of the ancients and the moderns. Starting with the French writer Fontenelle, it was taken up in England by Sir William Temple (*Essay upon Ancient and Modern Learning,* 1692) and involved, among others, Jonathan Swift (*Battle of the Books,* 1704) and the celebrated Cambridge classical scholar, Richard Bentley.—F. W. G.

the limited conception which many educational reformers have formed to themselves of a human being's power of acquisition.[8] The study of science, they truly say, is indispensable; our present education neglects it (there is truth in this too, though it is not all truth); and they think it impossible to find room for the studies which they desire to encourage but by turning out, at least from general education, those which are now chiefly cultivated. How absurd, they say, that the whole of boyhood should be taken up in acquiring an imperfect knowledge of two dead languages. Absurd indeed; but is the human mind's capacity to learn measured by that of Eton and Westminster to teach?[9] I should prefer to see these reformers pointing their attacks against the shameful inefficiency of the schools, public and private, which pretend to teach these two languages and do not. I should like to hear them denounce the wretched methods of teaching and the criminal idleness and supineness which waste the entire boyhood of the pupils without really giving to most of them more than a smattering, if even that, of the only kind of knowledge which is even pretended to be cared for. Let us try what conscientious and intelligent teaching can do, before we presume to decide what cannot be done.

[8] Perhaps Mill was misled by his own extraordinary intellectual powers into overestimating those of others—though, as he goes on to say, much time could be saved by more efficient teaching.—F. W. G.

[9] Complaints against the ineffectiveness of classics teaching and the consequent waste of children's time recur through the history of English education; for instance: Sir Thomas Elyot, *The Governour* (1531): "And by that time he cometh to the most swete and pleasant redinge of olde autours, the sparke of fervent desire of lernynge is extincte with the burdone of grammar" (Everyman edition; London: Dent, 1907, p. 35); John Milton, *Tractate of Education* (1644): "We do amiss to spend seven or eight years

Scotland has on the whole, in this respect, been considerably more fortunate than England. Scotch youths have never found it impossible to leave school or the university having learnt somewhat of other things besides Greek and Latin; and why? Because Greek and Latin have been better taught. A beginning of classical instruction has all along been made in the common schools; and the common schools of Scotland, like her universities, have never been the mere shams that the English universities were during the last century and the greater part of the English classical schools still are. The only tolerable Latin grammars for school purposes that I know of, which had been produced in these islands until very lately, were written by Scotchmen.[10] Reason, indeed, is beginning to find its way by gradual infiltration even into English schools and to maintain a contest, though as yet a very unequal one, against routine.

---

merely in scraping together so much miserable Latin and Greek as might be learnt otherwise easily and delightfully in one year" (ed. E. E. Morris; London: Macmillan, 1895, p. 5); William Hazlitt, "On the Ignorance of the Learned" (1818): "Anyone who has passed through the regular gradations of a classical education, and is not made a fool by it, may consider himself as having had a very narrow escape" (in *Selected Essays,* ed. G. Keynes; New York: Random House, 1946, p. 15); Sir Thomas Wyse, arguing in his *Education Reform* (1836) for the inclusion of a wider range of studies in the curriculum writes: ". . . by a better arrangement of the period for commencing the classical languages, and by a better process in teaching them, not only time might easily be spared for these studies without interfering with that of the languages, but . . . in fact the languages themselves would gain instead of losing. . . ." Eton and Westminster were, of course (and still are) strongholds of classical teaching.—F. W. G.

[10] These included grammars by Andrew Simpson of Dunbar (1587) and Alexander Hume, the latter of which was prescribed for school use by the Scottish Parliament in 1612. These and all others, however, were superseded by Thomas Ruddiman's *Rudiments of the Latin Tongue* (1714), which became the standard grammar in Scottish schools for generations.—F. W. G.

A few practical reformers of school tuition, of whom Arnold[11] was the most eminent, have made a beginning of amendment in many things; but reforms worthy of the name are always slow; and reform even of governments and churches is not so slow as that of schools, for there is the great preliminary difficulty of fashioning the instruments—of teaching the teachers. If all the improvements in the mode of teaching languages, which are already sanctioned by experience, were adopted into our classical schools, we should soon cease to hear of Latin and Greek as studies which must engross the school years and render impossible any other acquirements. If a boy learnt Greek and Latin on the same principle on which a mere child learns with such ease and rapidity any modern language, namely, by acquiring some familiarity with the vocabulary by practice and repetition before being troubled with grammatical rules[12]—those rules being acquired with tenfold greater facility when the cases to which they apply are already familiar to the mind—an average schoolboy, long before the age at which schooling terminates, would be able to read fluently and with intelligent interest any ordinary Latin or Greek author in prose or verse, would have a competent knowledge of the grammatical structure of both languages, and have had time besides for an ample amount of scientific instruction. I might go much further; but I am as unwilling to speak out all that I think practicable in this matter as George Stephenson was

[11] Thomas Arnold, headmaster of Rugby School.—F. W. G.

[12] Cf. John Locke, *Some Thoughts Concerning Education* (1693), § 165, who recommends "to trouble the child with no grammar at all, but to have Latin, as English has been, without the perplexity of rules, talked into him." Locke and Mill would have approved, no doubt, of current audiovisual methods of teaching Latin.—F. W. G.

about railways, when he calculated the average speed of a train at ten miles an hour, because, if he had estimated it higher, the practical men would have turned a deaf ear to him as that most unsafe character in their estimation, an enthusiast and a visionary. The results have shown, in that case, who was the real practical man. What the results would show in the other case, I will not attempt to anticipate. But I will say confidently that, if the two classical languages were properly taught, there would be no need whatever for ejecting them from the school course in order to have sufficient time for everything else that need be included therein.

Let me say a few words more on this strangely limited estimate of what it is possible for human beings to learn, resting on a tacit assumption that they are already as efficiently taught as they ever can be. So narrow a conception not only vitiates our idea of education, but actually, if we receive it, darkens our anticipations as to the future progress of mankind. For if the inexorable conditions of human life make it useless for one man to attempt to know more than one thing, what is to become of the human intellect as facts accumulate? In every generation, and now more rapidly than ever, the things which it is necessary that somebody should know are more and more multiplied. Every department of knowledge becomes so loaded with details, that one who endeavours to know it with minute accuracy must confine himself to a smaller and smaller portion of the whole extent; every science and art must be cut up into subdivisions, until each man's portion, the district which he thoroughly knows, bears about the same ratio to the whole range of useful knowledge that the art of putting on a pin's head does to the field of human industry.

Now if, in order to know that little completely, it is necessary to remain wholly ignorant of all the rest, what will soon be the worth of a man for any human purpose except his own infinitesimal fraction of human wants and requirements? His state will be even worse than that of simple ignorance. Experience proves that there is no one study or pursuit which, practised to the exclusion of all others, does not narrow and pervert the mind, breeding in it a class of prejudices special to that pursuit, besides a general prejudice, common to all narrow specialities, against large views from an incapacity to take in and appreciate the grounds of them. We should have to expect that human nature would be more and more dwarfed and unfitted for great things by its very proficiency in small ones. But matters are not so bad with us; there is no ground for so dreary an anticipation. It is not the utmost limit of human acquirement to know only one thing, but to combine a minute knowledge of one or a few things with a general knowledge of many things. By a general knowledge I do not mean a few vague impressions. An eminent man, one of whose writings is part of the course of this University, Archbishop Whateley,[13] has well discriminated between a general knowledge and a superficial knowledge. To have a general knowledge of a subject is to know only its leading truths, but to know these not superficially but thoroughly, so as to have a true conception of the subject in its great features, leaving the minor details to those who require them for the purposes of their special pursuit.

[13] Richard Whateley, Fellow of Oriel College, Oxford, and later Archbishop of Dublin. The book referred to is his *Elements of Logic* (1826), reviewed by Mill in *The Westminster Review,* January 1828.—F. W. G.

There is no incompatibility between knowing a wide range of subjects up to this point and some one subject with the completeness required by those who make it their principal occupation. It is this combination which gives an enlightened public: a body of cultivated intellects, each taught by its attainments in its own province what real knowledge is, and knowing enough of other subjects to be able to discern who are those that know them better. The amount of knowledge is not to be lightly estimated which qualifies us for judging to whom we may have recourse for more. The elements of the more important studies being widely diffused, those who have reached the higher summits find a public capable of appreciating their superiority and prepared to follow their lead. It is thus too that minds are formed capable of guiding and improving public opinion on the greater concerns of practical life. Government and civil society are the most complicated of all subjects accessible to the human mind; and he who would deal competently with them as a thinker, and not as a blind follower of a party, requires not only a general knowledge of the leading facts of life, both moral and material, but an understanding exercised and disciplined in the principles and rules of sound thinking up to a point which neither the experience of life nor any one science or branch of knowledge affords. Let us understand, then, that it should be our aim in learning, not merely to know the one thing which is to be our principal occupation as well as it can be known, but to do this and also to know something of all the great subjects of human interest: taking care to know that something accurately; marking well the dividing line between what we know accurately and what we do not; and remembering that our object should be to obtain a true view of nature and life in their broad outline, and that it is idle to throw away time upon the details of anything which is to form no part of the occupation of our practical energies.

It by no means follows, however, that every useful branch of general, as distinct from professional, knowledge should be included in the curriculum of school or university studies. There are things which are better learnt out of school, or when the school years, and even those usually passed in a Scottish university, are over. I do not agree with those reformers who would give a regular and prominent place in the school or university course to modern languages. This is not because I attach small importance to the knowledge of them. No one can in our age be esteemed a well-instructed person who is not familiar with at least the French language, so as to read French books with ease; and there is great use in cultivating a familiarity with German. But living languages are so much more easily acquired by intercourse with those who use them in daily life;[14] a few months in the country itself, if properly employed, go so much farther than as many years of school lessons, that it is really waste of time for those to whom that easier mode is attainable to labour at them with no help but that of books and masters; and it will in time be made attainable through international schools and colleges to many more than at present. Universities do enough to facilitate the study of modern languages if they give a mastery over that ancient language which is the foundation of most of them and the possession of which makes it easier to learn four or five of the continental languages than it is to learn one of them without it.[15] Again, it has

[14] This is how Mill himself learned French; he spent a year in France at the age of fourteen.—F. W. G.

[15] Latin, the parent tongue of French, Italian, Spanish and Por-

always seemed to me a great absurdity that history and geography should be taught in schools, except in elementary schools for the children of the labouring classes, whose subsequent access to books is limited. Who ever really learnt history and geography except by private reading? And what an utter failure a system of education must be, if it has not given the pupil a sufficient taste for reading to seek for himself those most attractive and easily intelligible of all kinds of knowledge. Besides, such history and geography as can be taught in schools exercise none of the faculties of the intelligence except the memory.[16] A university is indeed the place where the student should be introduced to the philosophy of history; where professors who not merely know the facts but have exercised their minds on them should initiate him into the causes and explanation, so far as within our reach, of the past life of mankind in its principal features. Historical criticism also—the tests of historical truth—are a subject to which his attention may well be drawn in this stage of his education. But of the mere facts of history, as commonly accepted, what educated youth of any mental activity does not learn as much as is necessary, if he is simply turned loose into an historical library? What he needs on this and on most other matters of common information is not that he should be taught it in boyhood, but that abundance of books should be accessible to him.

The only languages, then, and the only literature to which I would allow a place in the ordinary curriculum are those of the Greeks and Romans; and to these I

---

tuguese, and a constituent part of most other European languages.—F. W. G.

[16] Mill's comment no doubt reflects contemporary methods of teaching these subjects; it is wholly unacceptable today.—F. W. G.

would preserve the position in it which they at present occupy. That position is justified by the great value in education of knowing well some other cultivated language and literature than one's own, and by the peculiar value of those particular languages and literatures.

There is one purely intellectual benefit from a knowledge of languages, which I am specially desirous to dwell on. Those who have seriously reflected on the causes of human error have been deeply impressed with the tendency of mankind to mistake words for things. Without entering into the metaphysics of the subject we know how common it is to use words glibly and with apparent propriety, and to accept them confidently when used by others, without ever having had any distinct conception of the things denoted by them. To quote again from Archbishop Whateley, it is the habit of mankind to mistake familiarity for accurate knowledge. As we seldom think of asking the meaning of what we see every day, so when our ears are used to the sound of a word or phrase, we do not suspect that it conveys no clear idea to our minds and that we should have the utmost difficulty in defining it or expressing in any other words what we think we understand by it. Now it is obvious in what manner this bad habit tends to be corrected by the practice of translating with accuracy from one language to another and hunting out the meanings expressed in a vocabulary with which we have not grown familiar by early and constant use. I hardly know any greater proof of the extraordinary genius of the Greeks than that they were able to make such brilliant achievements in abstract thought knowing, as they generally did, no language but their own. But the Greeks did not escape the effects of this deficiency. Their greatest intellects, those who laid the foundation of philosophy and of all our intellectual culture, Plato and Aristotle, are continually led away by words, mistaking the accidents of language for real relations in nature and supposing that things which have the same name in the Greek tongue must be the same in their own essence. There is a well-known saying of Hobbes, the far-reaching significance of which you will more and more appreciate in proportion to the growth of your own intellect: "Words are the counters of wise men, but the money of fools."[17] With the wise man a word stands for the fact which it represents; to the fool it is itself the fact. To carry on Hobbes' metaphor, the counter is far more likely to be taken for merely what it is by those who are in the habit of using many different kinds of counters. But besides the advantage of possessing another cultivated language, there is a further consideration equally important. Without knowing the language of a people we never really know their thoughts, their feelings and their type of character; and unless we do possess this knowledge of some other people than ourselves, we remain to the hour of our death with our intellects only half expanded.[18] Look at a youth who has never been out of his family circle: he never dreams of any other opinions or ways of thinking than those he has been bred up in; or, if he has heard of any such, attributes them to some moral defect or inferiority of nature or education. If his family are Tory, he cannot conceive the possibility of being a Liberal; if Liberal, of being a Tory. What the notions and habits of a single family are to a boy who has had no intercourse beyond it, the no-

[17] *Leviathan I,* iv: "For words are wise men's counters, they do but reckon by them; but they are the money of fools" (ed. M. Oakeshott; London: Blackwell, 1947, p. 22).

[18] This is indeed one of the strongest arguments for learning a foreign language.—F. W. G.

tions and habits of his own country are to him who is ignorant of every other. Those notions and habits are to him human nature itself; whatever varies from them is an unaccountable aberration which he cannot mentally realise; the idea that any other ways can be right, or as near an approach to right as some of his own, is inconceivable to him. This does not merely close his eyes to the many things which every country still has to learn from others; it hinders every country from reaching the improvement which it could otherwise attain by itself. We are not likely to correct any of our opinions or mend any of our ways, unless we begin by conceiving that they are capable of amendment; but merely to know that foreigners think differently from ourselves, without understanding why they do so or what they really do think, does but confirm us in our self-conceit and connect our national vanity with the preservation of our own peculiarities. Improvement consists in bringing our opinions into nearer agreement with facts; and we shall not be likely to do this while we look at facts only through glasses coloured by those very opinions. But since we cannot divest ourselves of preconceived notions, there is no known means of eliminating their influence but by frequently using the differently coloured glasses of other people; and those of other nations, as the most different, are the best.

But if it is so useful on this account to know the language and literature of any other cultivated and civilised people, the most valuable of all to us in this respect are the languages and literature of the ancients. No nations of modern and civilised Europe are so unlike one another as the Greeks and Romans are unlike all of us, yet without being, as some remote Orientals are, so totally dissimilar that the labour of a life is required to enable us to understand them. Were this the only gain to be derived from a knowledge of the ancients, it would already place the study of them in a high rank among enlightening and liberalising pursuits. It is of no use saying that we may know them through modern writings. We may know something of them in that way; which is much better than knowing nothing. But modern books do not teach us ancient thought; they teach us some modern writer's notion of ancient thought. Modern books do not show us the Greeks and Romans; they tell us some modern writer's opinions about the Greeks and Romans. Translations are scarcely better. When we want really to know what a person thinks or says, we seek it at first hand from himself. We do not trust to another person's impression of his meaning, given in another person's words; we refer to his own. Much more is it necessary to do so when his words are in one language and those of his reporter in another. Modern phraseology never conveys the exact meaning of a Greek writer; it cannot do so except by a diffuse explanatory circumlocution which no translator dares use. We must be able, in a certain degree, to think in Greek, if we would represent to ourselves how a Greek thought; and this not only in the abstruse region of metaphysics, but about the political, religious and even domestic concerns of life.[19] I will mention a further aspect of this question, which, though I have not the merit of originating it, I do not remember to have seen noticed in any book. There is no part of our knowledge which it is more useful to obtain

[19] This is a powerful argument for encouraging at least a small number of students to acquire the Greek and Latin languages; without such classical scholars the task of reinterpreting to successive generations the heritage of Greece and Rome would cease and our civilization would be the poorer.—F. W. G.

at first hand—to go to the fountain-head for—than our knowledge of history. Yet this, in most cases, we hardly ever do. Our conception of the past is not drawn from its own records, but from books written about it, containing not the facts, but a view of the facts which has shaped itself in the mind of somebody of our own or a very recent time. Such books are very instructive and valuable; they help us to understand history, to interpret history, to draw just conclusions from it; at the worst they set us the example of trying to do all this; but they are not themselves history. The knowledge they give is upon trust, and even when they have done their best, it is not only incomplete but partial, because confined to what a few modern writers have seen in the materials and have thought worth picking out from among them. How little we learn of our own ancestors from Hume or Hallam or Macaulay,[20] compared with what we know if we add to what these tell us even a little reading of contemporary authors and documents! The most recent historians are so well aware of this that they fill their pages with extracts from the original materials, feeling that these extracts are the real history and their comments and thread of narrative are only helps towards understanding it. Now it is part of the great worth to us of our Greek and Latin studies that in them we do read history in the original sources. We are in actual contact with the contemporary minds; we are not dependent on hearsay; we have something by which we can test and check the representations and theories of modern historians. It may be asked, why then not study the original

[20] David Hume, *History of England* (6 vols., 1754–1762); Henry Hallam, *Constitutional History of England* (1827); Thomas Babington Macaulay, *History of England* (Vols. I and II, 1848; Vols. III and IV, 1855).—F. W. G.

materials of modern history? I answer, it is highly desirable to do so; and let me remark by the way that even this requires a dead language; nearly all the documents prior to the Reformation, and many subsequent to it, being written in Latin. But the exploration of these documents, though a most useful pursuit, cannot be a branch of education. Not to speak of their vast extent and the fragmentary nature of each, the strongest reason is that in learning the spirit of our own past ages, until a comparatively recent period, from contemporary writers we learn hardly anything else. Those authors, with a few exceptions, are little worth reading on their own account. While in studying the great writers of antiquity we are not only learning to understand the ancient mind, but laying in a stock of wise thought and observation still valuable to ourselves; and at the same time making ourselves familiar with a number of the most perfect and finished literary compositions which the human mind has produced—compositions which, from the altered conditions of human life, are likely to be seldom paralleled in their sustained excellence by the times to come.

Even as mere languages, no modern European language is so valuable a discipline to the intellect as those of Greece and Rome on account of their regular and complicated structure. Consider for a moment what grammar is. It is the most elementary part of logic.[21] It is the beginning of the analysis of the thinking process. The principles and rules of grammar are the means by

[21] The relation between grammar and logic is not so close as Mill here assumes. Grammar is primarily *descriptive;* it shows how language is used in actual discourse. Logic is *normative;* it *prescribes* how thought must proceed if its conclusions are to be valid. But the evident relationship between language and thought implies a common ground which grammar and logic both share.—F. W. G.

which the forms of language are made to correspond with the universal forms of thought. The distinctions between the various parts of speech, between the cases of nouns, the moods and tenses of verbs, the functions of particles, are distinctions in thought, not merely in words. Single nouns and verbs express objects and events, many of which can be cognised by the senses; but the modes of putting nouns and verbs together express the relations of objects and events, which can be cognised only by the intellect; and each different mode corresponds to a different relation. The structure of every sentence is a lesson in logic. The various rules of syntax oblige us to distinguish between the subject and predicate of a proposition, between the agent, the action, and the thing acted upon; to mark when an idea is intended to modify or qualify, or merely to unite with, some other idea; what assertions are categorical, what only conditional; whether the intention is to express similarity or contrast, to make a plurality of assertions conjunctively or disjunctively; what portions of a sentence, though grammatically complete within themselves, are mere members or subordinate parts of the assertion made by the entire sentence. Such things form the subject-matter of universal grammar; and the languages which teach it best are those which have the most definite rules and which provide distinct forms for the greatest number of distinctions in thought, so that if we fail to attend precisely and accurately to any of these, we cannot avoid committing a solecism in language. In these qualities the classical languages have an incomparable superiority over every modern language and over all languages, dead or living, which have a literature worth being generally studied.

But the superiority of the literature itself for purposes of education is still more marked and decisive. Even in the substantial value of the matter of which it is the vehicle it is very far from having been superseded. The discoveries of the ancients in science have been greatly surpassed, and as much of them as is still valuable loses nothing by being incorporated in modern treatises; but what does not so well admit of being transferred bodily, and has been very imperfectly carried off even piecemeal, is the treasure which they accumulated of what may be called the wisdom of life: the rich store of experience of human nature and conduct which the acute and observing minds of those ages, aided in their observations by the greater simplicity of manners and life, consigned to their writings and most of which retains all its value. The speeches in Thucydides, the *Rhetoric, Ethics* and *Politics* of Aristotle; the *Dialogues* of Plato; the *Orations* of Demosthenes; the *Satires* and especially the *Epistles* of Horace; all the writings of Tacitus; the great work of Quintilian,[22] a repertory of the best thoughts of the ancient world on all subjects connected with education; and, in a less formal manner, all that is left to us of the ancient historians, orators, philosophers and even dramatists are replete with remarks and maxims of singular good sense and penetration applicable both to political and to private life; and the actual truths we find in them are even surpassed in value by the encouragement and help they give us in the pursuit of truth. Human invention has never produced anything so valuable, in the way both of stimulation and of discipline to the inquiring intellect, as the dialectics of the ancients, of which many of the works of Aristotle illustrate the theory and those of Plato exhibit the practice.[23] No modern writings come

[22] On these Greek and Roman writers see above, pp. 134 ff.—F. W. G.

[23] Mill writes at some length on "dialectics" and its value in

near to these in teaching, both by precept and example, the way to investigate truth on those subjects so vastly important to us which remain matters of controversy from the difficulty or impossibility of bringing them to a directly experimental test. To question all things; never to turn away from any difficulty; to accept no doctrine either from ourselves or from other people without a rigid scrutiny by negative criticism, letting no fallacy or incoherence or confusion of thought slip by unperceived; above all, to insist upon having the meaning of a word clearly understood before using it, and the meaning of a proposition before assenting to it; these are the lessons we learn from the ancient dialecticians. With all this vigorous management of the negative element, they inspire no scepticism about the reality of truth or indifference to its pursuit. The noblest enthusiasm both for the search after truth and for applying it to its highest uses pervades these writers, Aristotle no less than Plato, though Plato has incomparably the greater power of imparting those feelings to others. In cultivating, therefore, the ancient languages as our best literary education we are all the while laying an admirable foundation for ethical and philosophical culture. In purely literary excellence—in perfection of form—the pre-eminence of the ancients is not disputed. In every department which they attempted, and they attempted almost all, their composition, like their sculpture, has been to the greatest modern artists an example, to be looked up to with hopeless ad-

---

his review of George Grote's *Plato and the Other Companions of Socrates (The Edinburgh Review,* April 1866; reprinted in *Dissertations and Discussions,* Vol. III). For Plato, he explains, dialectics consists in (a) "the testing every opinion by a negative scrutiny" and (b) "the direct search for the common feature of things that are classed together, . . . for the meaning of the class name" (pp. 320–321). Cf. *Autobiography,* pp. 58–59.—F. W. G.

miration but of inappreciable value as a light on high guiding their own endeavours. In prose and in poetry, in epic, lyric or dramatic as in historical, philosophical and oratorical art, the pinnacle on which they stand is equally eminent. I am now speaking of the form, the artistic perfection of treatment; for as regards substance I consider modern poetry to be superior to ancient in the same manner, though in a less degree, as modern science; it enters deeper into nature. The feelings of the modern mind are more various, more complex and manifold than those of the ancients ever were. The modern mind is, what the ancient mind was not, brooding and self-conscious; and its meditative self-consciousness has discovered depths in the human soul which the Greeks and Romans did not dream of and would not have understood.[24] But what they had got to express, they expressed in a manner which few even of the greatest moderns have seriously attempted to rival. It must be remembered that they had more time and that they wrote chiefly for a select class possessed of leisure. To us who write in a hurry for people who read in a hurry the attempt to give an equal degree of finish would be loss of time. But to be familiar with perfect models is not the less important to us because the element in which we work precludes even the effort to equal them. They show us at least what excellence is and make us desire it and strive to get as near to it as is within our reach. And this is the value to us of the ancient writers, all the more emphatically because their excellence does not admit of being copied or directly imitated. It does not consist in a trick which can be learnt, but in the per-

[24] It is noteworthy that Mill found consolation during his period of mental distress, not in the classical poets, but in Wordsworth.—F. W. G.

fect adaptation of means to ends. The secret of the style of the great Greek and Roman authors is that it is the perfection of good sense. In the first place, they never use a word without a meaning or a word which adds nothing to the meaning. They always (to begin with) had a meaning; they knew what they wanted to say; and their whole purpose was to say it with the highest degree of exactness and completeness and bring it home to the mind with the greatest possible clearness and vividness. It never entered into their thoughts to conceive of a piece of writing as beautiful in itself, abstractedly from what it had to express; its beauty must all be subservient to the most perfect expression of the sense. The *curiosa felicitas*[25] which their critics ascribed in a pre-eminent degree to Horace expresses the standard at which they all aimed. Their style is exactly described by Swift's definition, "the right words in the right places."[26] Look at an oration of Demosthenes: there is nothing in it which calls attention to itself as style at all; it is only after a close examination we perceive that every word is what it should be and where it should be, to lead the hearer smoothly and imperceptibly into the state of mind which the orator wishes to produce. The perfection of the workmanship is only visible in the total absence of any blemish or fault and of anything which checks the flow of thought and feeling, anything which even momentarily distracts the mind from the main purpose. But then (as has been well said) it was not the object of Demosthenes to make the Athenians cry out

[25] Petronius, *Satyricon*, 29, 118; a well-nigh untranslatable phrase which suggests a combination of assiduity, precision, and felicitous ingenuity.—F. W. G.

[26] "Proper words in proper places." Samuel Johnson's life of Jonathan Swift in *Lives of the English Poets* (Everyman edition; London: Dent, 1925), Vol. II, p. 273.—F. W. G.

"What a splendid speaker!" but to make them say "Let us march against Philip!" It was only in the decline of ancient literature that ornament began to be cultivated merely as ornament. In the time of its maturity not the merest epithet was put in because it was thought beautiful in itself; nor even for a merely descriptive purpose, for epithets purely descriptive were one of the corruptions of style which abound in Lucan,[27] for example; the word had no business there unless it brought out some feature which was wanted and helped to place the object in the light which the purpose of the composition required. These conditions being complied with, then indeed the intrinsic beauty of the means used was a source of additional effect of which it behoved them to avail themselves, like rhythm and melody of versification. But these great writers knew that ornament for the sake of ornament, ornament which attracts attention to itself and shines by its own beauties, only does so by calling off the mind from the main object, and thus not only interferes with the higher purpose of human discourse (which ought, and generally professes, to have some matter to communicate apart from the mere excitement of the moment), but also spoils the perfection of the composition as a piece of fine art by destroying the unity of effect. This, then, is the first great lesson in composition to be learnt from the classical authors. The second is, not to be prolix. In a single paragraph Thucydides can give a clear and vivid representation of a battle, such as a reader who has once taken it into his mind can seldom forget. The most powerful and affecting piece of narrative perhaps in all historical literature is the account of

[27] Marcanus Annaeus Lucanus, a Roman poet of the first century A.D.; his epic poem, *Pharsalia,* describes the war between Julius Caesar and Pompey—F. W. G.

the Sicilian catastrophe in his seventh book; yet how few pages does it fill![28] The ancients were concise because of the extreme pains they took with their compositions; almost all moderns are prolix because they do not. The great ancients could express a thought so perfectly in a few words or sentences that they did not need to add any more; the moderns, because they cannot bring it out clearly and completely at once, return again and again, heaping sentence upon sentence, each adding a little more elucidation, in hopes that though no single sentence expresses the full meaning, the whole together may give a sufficient notion of it. In this respect I am afraid we are growing worse instead of better, for want of time and patience and from the necessity we are in of addressing almost all writings to a busy and imperfectly prepared public. The demands of modern life are such, the work to be done, the mass to be worked upon are so vast, that those who have anything particular to say—who have, as the phrase goes, any message to deliver—cannot afford to devote their time to the production of masterpieces. But they would do far worse than they do, if there had never been masterpieces or if they had never known them. Early familiarity with the perfect makes our most imperfect production far less bad than it otherwise would be. To have a high standard of excellence often makes the whole difference of rendering our work good when it would otherwise be mediocre.

For all these reasons I think it important to retain these two languages and literatures in the place they oc-

[28] This was the disastrous conclusion (413 B.C.) of the Athenian attempt to besiege the Sicilian town of Syracuse; themselves besieged in turn, the Athenians attempted to break out but were forced to surrender. In captivity they were cruelly treated save for some few who could please their captors by reciting from the plays of Euripides.—F. W. G.

cupy as a part of liberal education, that is, of the education of all who are not obliged by their circumstances to discontinue their scholastic studies at a very early age. But the same reasons which vindicate the place of classical studies in general education show also the proper limitation of them. They should be carried as far as is sufficient to enable the pupil in after life to read the great works of ancient literature with ease. Those who have leisure and inclination to make scholarship or ancient history or general philology their pursuit of course require much more, but there is no room for more in general education. The laborious idleness in which the school-time is wasted away in the English classical schools deserves the severest reprehension. To what purpose should the most precious years of early life be irreparably squandered in learning to write bad Latin and Greek verses?[29] I do not see that we are much the better even for those who end by writing good ones. I am often tempted to ask the favourites of nature and fortune whether all the serious and important work of the world is done, that their time and energy can be spared for these *nugae difficiles*.[30] I am not blind to the utility of composing in a language as a means of learning it accurately. I hardly know any other means equally effectual. But why should not prose composition suffice? What need is there of original composition at all?—if that can be called original which unfortunate schoolboys, without any thoughts to express, hammer out on compulsion from mere memory, acquiring the pernicious habit

[29] This was Locke's view too: "Reading the excellent Greek and Roman poets is of more use than making bad verses of his own in a language that is not his own" *(Some Thoughts concerning Education,* § 174). See also the attack on verse-making by F. W. Farrar in *Essays on a Liberal Education* (1867), ch. 5.—F. W. G.

[30] "Tedious trifles."

which a teacher should consider it one of his first duties to repress, that of merely stringing together borrowed phrases. The exercise in composition most suitable to the requirements of learners is that most valuable one of retranslating from translated passages of a good author;[31] and to this might be added what still exists in many continental places of education, occasional practice in talking Latin. There would be something to be said for the time spent in the manufacture of verses, if such practice were necessary for the enjoyment of ancient poetry; though it would be better to lose that enjoyment than to purchase it at so extravagant a price. But the beauties of a great poet would be a far poorer thing than they are, if they only impressed us through a knowledge of the technicalities of his art. The poet needed those technicalities; they are not necessary to us. They are essential for criticizing a poem, but not for enjoying it. All that is wanted is sufficient familiarity with the language for its meaning to reach us without any sense of effort and clothed with the associations on which the poet counted for producing his effect. Whoever has this familiarity and a practised ear can have as keen a relish of the music of Virgil and Horace as of Gray or Burns or Shelley, though he know not the metrical rules of a common Sapphic or Alcaic.[32] I do not say that these rules ought not to be taught, but I would have a class apart for them and would make the appropriate exercises an optional, not a compulsory, part of the school teaching.

[31] This technique seems to have been first recommended by the Roman writer, Pliny the Younger, in the first century A.D. He is quoted with approval by Roger Ascham in *The Scholemaster* (1570; ed. W. A. Wright; Cambridge: Cambridge University Press, 1904, pp. 244-246).

[32] Two of the meters used by the Greek and Roman lyric poets. —F. W. G.

Much more might be said respecting classical instruction and literary cultivation in general as a part of liberal education. But it is time to speak of the uses of scientific instruction, or rather its indispensable necessity, for it is recommended by every consideration which pleads for any high order of intellectual education at all.

The most obvious part of the value of scientific instruction, the mere information that it gives, speaks for itself. We are born into a world which we have not made, a world whose phenomena take place according to fixed laws, of which we do not bring any knowledge into the world with us. In such a world we are appointed to live, and in it all our work is to be done. Our whole working power depends on knowing the laws of the world—in other words, the properties of the things which we have to work with and to work among and to work upon. We may and do rely for the greater part of this knowledge on the few who in each department make its acquisition their main business in life. But unless an elementary knowledge of scientific truths is diffused among the public, they never know what is certain and what is not, or who are entitled to speak with authority and who are not; and they either have no faith at all in the testimony of science or are the ready dupes of charlatans and impostors. They alternate between ignorant distrust and blind, often misplaced, confidence. Besides, who is there who would not wish to understand the meaning of the common physical facts that take place under his eye? Who would not wish to know why a pump raises water, why a lever moves heavy weights, why it is hot at the tropics and cold at the poles, why the moon is sometimes dark and sometimes bright, what is the cause of the tides? Do we not feel that he who is totally ignorant of these things, let him be ever so skilled in a special profession, is not an educated man but an ignoramus? It is surely no small part of education to put us in intelligent possession of the most important and most universally interesting facts of the universe, so that the world which surrounds us may not be a sealed book to us, uninteresting because unintelligible. This, however, is but the simplest and most obvious part of the utility of science and the part which, if neglected in youth, may be the most easily made up for afterwards. It is more important to understand the value of scientific instruction as a training and disciplining process, to fit the intellect for the proper work of a human being. Facts are the materials of our knowledge, but the mind itself is the instrument; and it is easier to acquire facts than to judge what they prove and how, through the facts which we know, to get to those which we want to know.

The most incessant occupation of the human intellect throughout life is the ascertainment of truth.[33] We are always needing to know what is actually true about something or other. It is not given to us all to discover great general truths that are a light to all men and to future generations; though with a better general education the number of those who could do so would be far greater than it is. But we all require the ability to judge between the conflicting opinions which are offered to us as vital truths; to choose what doctrines we will receive in the matter of religion, for example; to judge whether

[33] In this paragraph Mill implies that there are different kinds or aspects of truth but without clearly distinguishing them. Mathematical truth (mainly deductive) is not identical with scientific truth (mainly inductive), and these two are different again from religious truth and moral truth, which involve elements of intuition and commitment in addition to reason and observation.—F. W. G.

we ought to be Tories, Whigs or Radicals,[34] or to what length it is our duty to go with each; to form a rational conviction on great questions of legislation and internal policy and on the manner in which our country should behave to dependencies and to foreign nations. And the need we have of knowing how to discriminate truth is not confined to the larger truths. All through life it is our most pressing interest to find out the truth about all the matters we are concerned with. If we are farmers, we want to find what will truly improve our soil; if merchants, what will truly influence the markets of our commodities; if judges or jurymen or advocates, who it was that truly did an unlawful act or to whom a disputed right truly belongs. Every time we have to make a new resolution or alter an old one in any situation in life, we shall go wrong unless we know the truth about the facts on which our resolution depends. Now however different these searches for truth may look and however unlike they really are in their subject-matter, the methods of getting at truth and the tests of truth are in all cases much the same. There are but two roads by which truth can be discovered: observation and reasoning (observation, of course, including experiment). We all observe and we all reason, and therefore, more or less successfully, we all ascertain truths; but most of us do it very ill and could not get on at all, were we not able to fall back on others who do it better. If we could not do it in any degree, we should be mere instruments in the hands of those who could; they would be able to reduce us to slavery. Then how shall we best learn to do this? By being shown the way in which it has already been

[34] Conservatives, Liberals, Reformers.—F. W. G.

successfully done. The processes by which truth is attained, reasoning and observation, have been carried to their greatest known perfection in the physical sciences. As classical literature furnishes the most perfect types of the art of expression, so do the physical sciences those of the art of thinking. Mathematics and its application to astronomy and natural philosophy are the most complete example of the discovery of truths by reasoning; experimental science, of their discovery by direct observation. In all these cases we know that we can trust the operation, because the conclusions to which it has led have been found true by subsequent trial. It is by the study of these, then, that we may hope to qualify ourselves for distinguishing truth in cases where there do not exist the same ready means of verification.

In what consists the principal and most characteristic difference between one human intellect and another? In their ability to judge correctly of evidence. Our direct perceptions of truth are so limited, we know so few things by immediate intuition or, as it used to be called, by simple apprehension, that we depend for almost all our valuable knowledge on evidence external to itself; and most of us are very unsafe hands at estimating evidence where an appeal cannot be made to actual eyesight. The intellectual part of our education has nothing more important to do than to correct or mitigate this almost universal infirmity, this summary and substance of nearly all purely intellectual weakness. To do this with effect needs all the resources which the most perfect system of intellectual training can command. Those resources, as every teacher knows, are but of three kinds: first, models, secondly, rules, thirdly, appropriate practice. The models of the art of estimating evidence are furnished by science; the rules are suggested by science; and the study of science is the most fundamental portion of the practice.

Take in the first instance mathematics.[35] It is chiefly from mathematics we realise the fact that there actually is a road to truth by means of reasoning; that anything real, and which will be found true when tried, can be arrived at by a mere operation of the mind. The flagrant abuse of mere reasoning in the days of the schoolmen, when men argued confidently to supposed facts of outward nature without properly establishing their premises or checking the conclusions by observation, created a prejudice in the modern, and especially in the English, mind against deductive reasoning altogether as a mode of investigation. The prejudice lasted long and was upheld by the misunderstood authority of Lord Bacon,[36] until the prodigious applications of mathematics to physical science, to the discovery of the laws of external nature, slowly and tardily restored the reasoning process to the place which belongs to it as a source of real knowledge. Mathematics, pure and applied, are still the great conclusive example of what can be done by reasoning. Mathematics also habituates us to several of the principal precautions for the safety of the process. Our first studies in geometry teach us two invaluable lessons. One is to lay down at the beginning in express and clear terms all the premises from which we intend to reason. The

[35] There are clear echoes of Descartes in this paragraph; see *Discourse on Method*, especially Section 2.—F. W. G.

[36] Francis Bacon, Baron Verulam, Viscount St. Albans (1561–1626): he attacked the traditional deductive logic of the medieval schoolmen on the grounds that it was "not nearly subtle enough to deal with nature" and that it relied exclusively on syllogistic reasoning, the validity of which was vitiated by the inadequacy of its premises. See below, p. 197, note.—F. W. G.

other is to keep every step in the reasoning distinct and separate from all the other steps and to make each step safe before proceeding to another, expressly stating to ourselves at every joint in the reasoning what new premise we there introduce. It is not necessary that we should do this at all times in all our reasonings. But we must be always able and ready to do it. If the validity of our argument is denied or if we doubt it ourselves, that is the way to check it. In this way we are often enabled to detect at once the exact place where paralogism[37] or confusion get in; and after sufficient practice we may be able to keep them out from the beginning. It is to mathematics, again, that we owe our first notion of a connected body of truth—truths which grow out of one another and hang together so that each implies all the rest, that no one of them can be questioned without contradicting another or others, until in the end it appears that no part of the system can be false unless the whole is so. Pure mathematics first gave us this conception; applied mathematics extends it to the realm of physical nature. Applied mathematics shows us that not only the truths of abstract number and extension, but the external facts of the universe, which we apprehend by our senses, form, at least in a large part of all nature, a web similarly held together. We are able, by reasoning from a few fundamental truths, to explain and predict the phenomena of material objects; and what is still more remarkable, the fundamental truths were themselves found out by reasoning; for they are not such as are obvious to the senses, but had to be inferred by a mathematical process from a mass of minute details which alone came within the direct reach of human observation. When Newton in

[37] Illogicality.—F. W. G.

this manner discovered the laws of the solar system, he created for all posterity the true idea of science. He gave the most perfect example we are ever likely to have of that union of reasoning and observation which, by means of facts that can be directly observed, ascends to laws which govern multitudes of other facts—laws which not only explain and account for what we see, but give us assurance beforehand of much that we do not see, much that we never could have found out by observation, though, having been found out, it is always verified by the result.

While mathematics and the mathematical sciences supply us with a typical example of the ascertainment of truth by reasoning, those physical sciences which are not mathematical, such as chemistry and purely experimental physics, show us in equal perfection the other mode of arriving at certain truth,[38] by observation in its most accurate form, that of experiment. The value of mathematics in a logical point of view is an old topic with mathematicians, and has even been insisted on so exclusively as to provoke a counter-exaggeration, of which a well-known essay by Sir William Hamilton is an example;[39] but the logical value of experimental science is comparatively a new subject, yet there is no intellec-

[38] Scientists do not now claim certainty for their generalizations; scientific "truths" are open-ended—they are acceptable, if the evidence supports them, until they have been refuted.—F. W. G.

[39] "On the Study of Mathematics as an Exercise of Mind" (*The Edinburgh Review,* January 1836). Hamilton wrote the essay to counter what he felt to be excessive claims for mathematics as a liberal study, such as were made by William Whewell in his *Thoughts on the Study of Mathematics as a Part of a Liberal Education* (1835). Hamilton was a celebrated Scottish philosopher who held the chair of logic and metaphysics at Edinburgh from 1836 to 1846; Whewell, a pioneer in the philosophy of science, was Professor of Moral Philosophy at Cambridge, 1838 to 1855.

tual discipline more important than that which the experimental sciences afford. Their whole occupation consists in doing well what all of us during the whole of life are engaged in doing for the most part badly. All men do not affect to be reasoners, but all profess and really attempt to draw inferences from experience; yet hardly anyone who has not been a student of the physical sciences sets out with any just idea of what the process of interpreting experience really is. If a fact has occurred once or oftener and another fact has followed it, people think they have got an experiment and are well on the road towards showing that the one fact is the cause of the other. If they did but know the immense amount of precaution necessary to a scientific experiment; with what sedulous care the accompanying circumstances are contrived and varied, so as to exclude every agency but that which is the subject of the experiment—or, when disturbing agencies cannot be excluded, the minute accuracy with which their influence is calculated and allowed for, in order that the residue may contain nothing but what is due to the one agency under examination;[40] if these things were attended to, people would be much less easily satisfied that their opinions have the evidence of experience; many popular notions and generalisations which are in all mouths would be thought a great deal less certain than they are supposed to be; but we should begin to lay the foundation of really experimental knowledge on things which are now the subjects of mere vague discussion, where one side finds as much to say and says it as confidently as another and each person's opinion is less determined by evidence than by his accidental interest or prepossession. In politics, for instance,

[40] Mill here echoes the account of scientific procedure which he elaborates in his *System of Logic* (1843).—F. W. G.

it is evident to whoever comes to the study from that of the experimental sciences that no political conclusions of any value for practice can be arrived at by direct experience. Such specific experience as we can have serves only to verify, and even that insufficiently, the conclusions of reasoning. Take any active force you please in politics, take the liberties of England, or free trade; how should we know that either of these things conduced to prosperity, if we could discern no tendency in the things themselves to produce it? If we had only the evidence of what is called our experience, such prosperity as we enjoy might be owing to a hundred other causes and might have been obstructed, not promoted, by these. All true political science is, in one sense of the phrase, *a priori,* being deduced from the tendencies of things, tendencies known either through our general experience of human nature or as the result of an analysis of the course of history considered as a progressive evolution. It requires, therefore, the union of induction and deduction, and the mind that is equal to it must have been well disciplined in both. But familiarity with scientific experiment at least does the useful service of inspiring a wholesome scepticism about the conclusions which the mere surface of experience suggests.

The study, on the one hand, of mathematics and its applications, on the other, of experimental science prepares us for the principal business of the intellect by the practice of it in the most characteristic cases and by familiarity with the most perfect and successful models of it. But in great things as in small, examples and models are not sufficient; we want rules as well. Familiarity with the correct use of a language in conversation and writing does not make rules of grammar unnecessary; nor does the amplest knowledge of sciences of reasoning and experiment dispense with rules of logic. We may have heard correct reasonings and seen skilful experiments all our lives; we shall not learn by mere imitation to do the like unless we pay careful attention to how it is done. It is much easier in these abstract matters than in purely mechanical ones to mistake bad work for good. To mark out the difference between them is the province of logic. Logic lays down the general principles and laws of the search after truth, the conditions which, whether recognised or not, must actually have been observed if the mind has done its work rightly. Logic is the intellectual complement of mathematics and physics: those sciences give the practice of which logic is the theory; it declares the principles, rules and precepts of which they exemplify the observance.

The science of logic has two parts, ratiocinative[41] and inductive logic. The one helps to keep us right in reasoning from premises, the other in concluding from observation. Ratiocinative logic is much older than inductive, because reasoning in the narrower sense of the word is an easier process than induction, and the science which works by mere reasoning, pure mathematics, had been carried to a considerable height while the sciences of observation were still in the purely empirical period. The principles of ratiocination, therefore, were the earliest understood and systematised, and the logic of ratiocination is even now suitable to an earlier stage in education than that of induction. The principles of induction cannot be properly understood without some previous study of the inductive sciences; but the logic of reasoning, which was already carried to a high degree of perfection by Aristotle, does not absolutely require even a knowl-

[41] Deductive.—F. W. G.

edge of mathematics, but can be sufficiently exemplified and illustrated from the practice of daily life.

Of logic I venture to say (even if limited to that of mere ratiocination, the theory of names, propositions and the syllogism) that there is no part of intellectual education which is of greater value or whose place can so ill be supplied by anything else. Its uses, it is true, are chiefly negative; its function is not so much to teach us to go right as to keep us from going wrong. But in the operations of the intellect it is so much easier to go wrong than right; it is so utterly impossible for even the most vigorous mind to keep itself in the path but by maintaining a vigilant watch against all deviations and noting all the byways by which it is possible to go astray —that the chief difference between one reasoner and another consists in their less or greater liability to be misled.

Logic points out all the possible ways in which, starting from true premises, we may draw false conclusions. By its analysis of the reasoning process and the forms it supplies for stating and setting forth our reasonings it enables us to guard the points at which a fallacy is in danger of slipping in or to lay our fingers upon the place where it has slipped in. When I consider how very simple the theory of reasoning is and how short a time is sufficient for acquiring a thorough knowledge of its principles and rules and even considerable expertness in applying them, I can find no excuse for omission to study it on the part of anyone who aspires to succeed in any intellectual pursuit. Logic is the great disperser of hazy and confused thinking; it clears up the fogs which hide from us our own ignorance and make us believe that we understand a subject when we do not. We must not be led away by talk about inarticulate giants who do great deeds without knowing how and see into the most recondite truths without any of the ordinary helps and without being able to explain to other people how they reach their conclusions, nor consequently to convince any other people of the truth of them. There may be such men, as there are deaf and dumb persons who do clever things, but for all that, speech and hearing are faculties by no means to be dispensed with. If you want to know whether you are thinking rightly, put your thoughts into words. In the very attempt to do this you will find yourselves, consciously or unconsciously, using logical forms. Logic compels us to throw our meaning into distinct propositions and our reasonings into distinct steps. It makes us conscious of all the implied assumptions on which we are proceeding and which, if not true, vitiate the entire process. It makes us aware what extent of doctrine we commit ourselves to by any course of reasoning, and obliges us to look the implied premises in the face and make up our minds whether we can stand to them. It makes our opinions consistent with themselves and with one another, and forces us to think clearly even when it cannot make us think correctly. It is true that error may be consistent and systematic as well as truth; but this is not the common case. It is no small advantage to see clearly the principles and consequences involved in our opinions and which we must either accept or else abandon those opinions. We are much nearer to finding truth when we search for it in broad daylight. Error, pursued rigorously to all that is implied in it, seldom fails to get detected by coming into collision with some known and admitted fact.

You will find abundance of people to tell you that logic is no help to thought and that people cannot be taught to think by rules. Undoubtedly rules by themselves, without practice, go but a little way in teaching anything. But if the practice of thinking is not improved by rules, I venture to say it is the only difficult thing done by human beings that is not so. A man learns to saw wood principally by practice, but there are rules for doing it grounded on the nature of the operation, and if he is not taught the rules, he will not saw well until he has discovered them for himself. Wherever there is a right way and a wrong, there must be a difference between them, and it must be possible to find out what the difference is; and when found out and expressed in words, it is a rule for the operation. If anyone is inclined to disparage rules, I say to them, try to learn anything which there are rules for without knowing the rules, and see how you succeed. To those who think lightly of the school logic[42] I say, take the trouble to learn it. You will easily do so in a few weeks, and you will see whether it is of no use to you in making your mind clear and keeping you from stumbling in the dark over the most outrageous fallacies. Nobody, I believe, who has really learnt it and who goes on using his mind, is insensible to its benefits, unless he started with a prejudice or, like some eminent English and Scottish thinkers of the past century, is under the influence of a reaction against the exaggerated pretensions made by the schoolmen not so much in behalf of logic as of the reasoning process itself. Still more highly must the use of logic be estimated if we include in it, as we ought to do, the principles and rules of induction as well as of ratiocination. As the one logic guards us against bad deduction, so does the other against bad generalisation, which is a still more universal error. If men easily err in arguing from one general

[42] The traditional logic of deduction and the syllogism.—F. W. G.

proposition to another, still more easily do they go wrong in interpreting the observations made by themselves and others. There is nothing in which an untrained mind shows itself more hopelessly incapable than in drawing the proper general conclusions from its own experience. And even trained minds, when all their training is on a special subject and does not extend to the general principles of induction, are only kept right when there are ready opportunities of verifying their inferences by facts. Able scientific men, when they venture upon subjects in which they have no facts to check them, are often found drawing conclusions or making generalisations from their experimental knowledge such as any sound theory of induction would show to be utterly unwarranted. So true is it that practice alone, even of a good kind, is not sufficient without principles and rules. Lord Bacon had the great merit of seeing that rules were necessary and conceiving to a very considerable extent their true character. The defects of his conception were such as were inevitable while the inductive sciences were only in the earliest stage of their progress and the highest efforts of the human mind in that direction had not yet been made.[43] Inadequate as the Baconian view of induction was and rapidly as the practice outgrew it, it is only within a generation or two that any considerable improvement has been made in the theory—very much through the impulse given by two of the many distinguished men who have adorned the Scottish universities, Dugald Stewart and Brown.[44]

[43] Mill criticizes Bacon's account of induction in his *System of Logic*, III, xxii and V, iii.—F. W. G.

[44] Dugald Stewart, Professor of Moral Philosophy at Edinburgh, 1785 to 1820. Thomas Brown was closely associated with Stewart and was jointly professor with him from 1810.—F. W. G.

I have given a very incomplete and summary view of the educational benefits derived from instruction in the more perfect sciences and in the rules for the proper use of the intellectual faculties which the practice of those sciences has suggested. There are other sciences which are in a more backward state and tax the whole powers of the mind in its mature years, yet a beginning of which may be beneficially made in university studies, while a tincture of them is valuable even to those who are never likely to proceed further. The first is physiology, the science of the laws of organic and animal life and especially of the structure and functions of the human body. It would be absurd to pretend that a profound knowledge of this difficult subject can be acquired in youth or as a part of general education. Yet an acquaintance with its leading truths is one of those acquirements which ought not to be the exclusive property of a particular profession. The value of such knowledge for daily uses has been made familiar to us by the sanitary discussions of late years.[45] There is hardly one among us who may not, in some position of authority, be required to form an opinion and take part in public action on sanitary subjects. And the importance of understanding the true conditions of health and disease, of knowing how to acquire and preserve that healthy habit of body which the most tedious and costly medical

[45] Health and sanitation were matters of great public concern and private endeavor in England during the middle years of the nineteenth century. In London and the major towns the conditions were, by modern standards, bad even for the rich; for the poor they were appalling. Tuberculosis was rife at the time; several of Mill's friends and family died of it, including his wife, Harriet; Mill himself contracted it but recovered (see Packe's *Life of John Stuart Mill*).

On the spelling of "sanitary" there is a letter of Mill's in *The Times,* April 7, 1847, signed "Orthographicus."—F. W. G.

treatment so often fails to restore when once lost, should secure a place in general education for the principal maxims of hygiene and some of those even of practical medicine. For those who aim at high intellectual cultivation the study of physiology has still greater recommendations and is, in the present state of advancement of the higher studies, a real necessity. The practice which it gives in the study of nature is such as no other physical science affords in the same kind and is the best introduction to the difficult questions of politics and social life. Scientific education, apart from professional objects, is but a preparation for judging rightly of Man and of his requirements and interests. But to this final pursuit, which has been called *par excellence* the proper study of mankind, physiology is the most serviceable of the sciences because it is the nearest. Its subject is already Man: the same complex and manifold being whose properties are not independent of circumstance and immovable from age to age, like those of the ellipse and hyperbola or of sulphur and phosphorus, but are infinitely various, indefinitely modifiable by art or accident, graduating by the nicest shades into one another and reacting upon one another in a thousand ways, so that they are seldom capable of being isolated and observed separately. With the difficulties of the study of a being so constituted the physiologist, and he alone among scientific enquirers, is already familiar. Take what view we will of man as a spiritual being, one part of his nature is far more like another than either of them is like anything else. In the organic world we study nature under disadvantages very similar to those which affect the study of moral and political phenomena; our means of making experiments are almost as limited, while the extreme complexity of the facts makes the conclusions of general reasoning unusually precarious on account of the vast number of circumstances that conspire to determine every result. Yet in spite of these obstacles it is found possible in physiology to arrive at a considerable number of well-ascertained and important truths. This therefore is an excellent school in which to study the means of overcoming similar difficulties elsewhere. It is in physiology too that we are first introduced to some of the conceptions which play the greatest part in the moral and social sciences, but which do not occur at all in those of inorganic nature—as, for instance, the idea of predisposition and of predisposing causes, as distinguished from exciting causes. The operation of all moral forces is immensely influenced by predisposition; without that element it is impossible to explain the commonest facts of history and social life. Physiology is also the first science in which we recognise the influence of habit—the tendency of something to happen again merely because it has happened before. From physiology, too, we get our clearest notion of what is meant by development or evolution. The growth of a plant or animal from the first germ is the typical specimen of a phenomenon which rules through the whole course of the history of man and society—increase of function through expansion and differentiation of structure by internal forces. I cannot enter into the subject at greater length; it is enough if I throw out hints which may be germs of further thought in yourselves. Those who aim at high intellectual achievements may be assured that no part of their time will be less wasted than that which they employ in becoming familiar with the methods and with the main conceptions of the science of organisation and life.

Physiology at its upper extremity touches on psychology or the philosophy of mind; and without raising any disputed questions about the limits between Matter and Spirit, the nerves and brain are admitted to have so intimate a connection with the mental operations, that the student of the last cannot dispense with a considerable knowledge of the first. The value of psychology itself need hardly be expatiated upon in a Scottish university; for it has always been there studied with brilliant success. Almost everything which has been contributed from these islands towards its advancement since Locke and Berkeley has until very lately, and much of it even in the present generation, proceeded from Scottish authors and Scottish professors.[46] Psychology, in truth, is simply the knowledge of the laws of human nature. If there is anything that deserves to be studied by man, it is his own nature and that of his fellow-men; and if it is worth studying at all, it is worth studying scientifically, so as to reach the fundamental laws which underlie and govern all the rest. With regard to the suitableness of this subject for general education a distinction must be made. There are certain observed laws of our thoughts and of our feelings which rest upon experimental evidence and, once seized, are a clue to the interpretation of much that we are conscious of in ourselves and observe in one another. Such, for example, are the laws of association.[47] Psychology, so far as it consists of such laws—I speak of the laws themselves, not of their disputed applications—is as positive and certain a science as chemistry, and fit

[46] Such as, for instance, David Hume, Dugald Stewart, Sir William Hamilton, Thomas Brown, James Mill, and Alexander Bain (the last, John Mill's friend and biographer, was professor of logic and English at Aberdeen, 1860 to 1880).

[47] On association psychology see the Introduction, pp. 19–20. Note the very interesting passage in the *Autobiography* (pp. 121–124), where Mill analyzes in terms of association psychology the failure of his own education to cultivate the feelings.—F. W. G.

to be taught as such. When, however, we pass beyond the bounds of these admitted truths to questions which are still in controversy among the different philosophical schools—how far the higher operations of the mind can be explained by association, how far we must admit other primary principles—what faculties of the mind are simple, what complex, and what is the composition of the latter—above all, when we embark upon the sea of metaphysics properly so called and enquire, for instance, whether time and space are real existences, as is our spontaneous impression, or forms of our sensitive faculty, as is maintained by Kant, or complex ideas generated by association; whether matter and spirit are conceptions merely relative to our faculties or facts existing *per se,* and in the latter case, what is the nature and limit of our knowledge of them; whether the will of man is free or determined by causes, and what is the real difference between the two doctrines (matters on which the most thinking men and those who have given most study to the subjects are still divided); it is neither to be expected nor desired that those who do not specially devote themselves to the higher departments of speculation should employ much of their time in attempting to get to the bottom of these questions. But it is a part of liberal education to know that such controversies exist and, in a general way, what has been said on both sides of them. It is instructive to know the failures of the human intellect as well as its successes, its imperfect as well as its perfect attainments; to be aware of the open questions as well as of those which have been definitively resolved. A very summary view of these disputed matters may suffice for the many; but a system of education is not intended solely for the many; it has to kindle the aspirations and aid the efforts of those who are destined to stand forth as thinkers above the multitude; and for these there is hardly to be found any discipline comparable to that which these metaphysical controversies afford. For they are essentially questions about the estimation of evidence; about the ultimate grounds of belief; the conditions required to justify our most familiar and intimate convictions; and the real meaning and import of words and phrases which we have used from infancy as if we understood all about them, which are even at the foundation of human language, yet of which no one except a metaphysician has rendered to himself a complete account. Whatever philosophical opinions the study of these questions may lead us to adopt, no one ever came out of the discussion of them without increased vigour of understanding, an increased demand for precision of thought and language, and a more careful and exact appreciation of the nature of proof. There never was any sharpener of the intellectual faculties superior to the Berkeleian controversy.[48] There is even now no reading more profitable to students—confining myself to writers in our own language, and notwithstanding that so many of their speculations are already obsolete—than Hobbes and Locke, Reid and Stewart, Hume, Hartley and Brown,[49] on condition that these great thinkers are not read passively, as masters to be followed, but actively, as supplying materials and incentives to thought. To come to our own contemporaries, he who has mastered Sir William Hamilton and your own lamented Ferrier as distinguished representatives of one of the two great schools

[48] George Berkeley, bishop and philosopher, held the paradoxical doctrine that "to exist is to be perceived" and that the external world exists, therefore, only in so far as it is perceived—by us or by God.—F. W. G.

[49] On these see above, pp. 142 ff.—F. W. G.

of philosophy, and an eminent professor in a neighbouring university, Professor Bain, probably the greatest living authority in the other,[50] has gained a practice in the most searching methods of philosophic investigation applied to the most arduous subjects, which is no inadequate preparation for any intellectual difficulties that he is ever likely to be called on to resolve.

In this brief outline of a complete scientific education I have said nothing about direct instruction in that which it is the chief of all the ends of intellectual education to qualify us for, the exercise of thought on the great interests of mankind as moral and social beings, ethics and politics in the largest sense. These things are not, in the existing state of human knowledge, the subject of a science generally admitted and accepted. Politics cannot be learnt once for all from a text-book or the instructions of a master. What we require to be taught on that subject is to be our own teachers. It is a subject on which we have no masters to follow; each must explore for himself and exercise an independent judgement. Scientific politics do not consist in having a set of conclusions ready made, to be applied everywhere indiscriminately, but in setting the mind to work in a scientific spirit to discover in each instance the truths applicable to the given case. And this, at present, scarcely any two persons do in the same way. Education is not entitled, on this subject, to recommend any set of opinions as resting on the authority of established science. But it can supply the student with materials for his own mind and with helps to use them. It can make him acquainted with the best speculations on the subject, taken from different points of view, none of which will

[50] On Hamilton see above, p. 190, note. James Ferrier was Professor of Moral Philosophy at St. Andrews, 1845 to 1864; with

be found complete, while each embodies some considerations really relevant, really requiring to be taken into account. Education may also introduce us to the principal facts which have a direct bearing on the subject, namely the different modes or stages of civilisation that have been found among mankind and the characteristic properties of each. This is the true purpose of historical studies as prosecuted in a university. The leading facts of ancient and modern history should be known by the student from his private reading; if that knowledge be wanting, it cannot possibly be supplied here. What a Professor of History has to teach is the meaning of those facts. His office is to help the student in collecting from history what are the main differences between human beings and between the institutions of society at one time or place and at another; in picturing to himself human life and the human conception of life as they were at the different stages of human development; in distinguishing between what is the same in all ages and what is progressive, and forming some incipient conception of the causes and laws of progress. All these things are as yet very imperfectly understood even by the most philosophic enquirers, and are quite unfit to be taught dogmatically. The object is to lead the student to attend to them, to make him take interest in history, not as a mere narrative, but as a chain of causes and effects still unwinding itself before his eyes and full of momentous consequences to himself and his descendants; the unfolding of a great epic or dramatic action, to terminate in the

---

Hamilton he adopted a metaphysical and idealist position in regard to problems of mind and knowledge. Bain's view, on the other hand, was rigorously scientific; he sought the solution of such problems in the study of the brain and nervous system.—F. W. G.

happiness or misery, the elevation or degradation, of the human race; an unremitting conflict between good and evil powers, of which every act done by any of us, insignificant as we are, forms one of the incidents; a conflict in which even the smallest of us cannot escape from taking part, in which whoever does not help the right side is helping the wrong, and for our share in which, whether it be greater or smaller, and let its actual consequences be visible or in the main invisible, no one of us can escape the responsibility. Though education cannot arm and equip its pupils for this fight with any complete philosophy either of politics or of history, there is much positive instruction that it can give them having a direct bearing on the duties of citizenship. They should be taught the outlines of the civil and political institutions of their own country, and in a more general way, of the more advanced of the other civilised nations. Those branches of politics or of the laws of social life in which there exists a collection of facts or thoughts sufficiently sifted and methodised to form the beginning of a science should be taught *ex professo*.[51] Among the chief of these is political economy, the sources and conditions of wealth and material prosperity for aggregate bodies of human beings. This study approaches nearer to the rank of a science, in the sense in which we apply that name to the physical sciences, than anything else connected with politics yet does. I need not enlarge on the important lessons which it affords for the guidance of life and for the estimation of laws and institutions, or on the necessity of knowing all that it can teach in order to have true views of the course of human affairs or form plans for their improvement which will stand actual trial. The

[51] "As a matter of personal conviction."—F. W. G.

same persons who cry down logic will generally warn you against political economy. It is unfeeling, they will tell you. It recognises unpleasant facts. For my part, the most unfeeling thing I know of is the law of gravitation; it breaks the neck of the best and most amiable person without scruple if he forgets for a single moment to give heed to it. The winds and waves too are very unfeeling. Would you advise those who go to sea to deny the winds and waves—or to make use of them and find the means of guarding against their dangers? My advice to you is to study the great writers on political economy and hold firmly by whatever in them you find true; and depend upon it that if you are not selfish or hard-hearted already, political economy will not make you so. Of no less importance than political economy is the study of what is called jurisprudence—the general principles of law; the social necessities which laws are required to meet; the features common to all systems of law, and the differences between them; the requisites of good legislation, the proper mode of constructing a legal system, and the best constitution of courts of justice and modes of legal procedure. These things are not only the chief part of the business of government, but the vital concern of every citizen; and their improvement affords a wide scope for the energies of any duly prepared mind, ambitious of contributing towards the better condition of the human race. For this, too, admirable helps have been provided by writers of our own or of a very recent time. At the head of them stands Bentham, undoubtedly the greatest master who ever devoted the labour of a life to let in light on the subject of law;[52] and who is the more

[52] Jeremy Bentham is now best remembered for his philosophy of ethical utilitarianism; but in his own time he was more important as a critic of law and judicial institutions. His *Introduc-*

intelligible to non-professional persons, because, as his way is, he builds up the subject from its foundation in the facts of human life and shows by careful consideration of ends and means what law might and ought to be, in deplorable contrast with what it is. Other enlightened jurists have followed with contributions of two kinds, as types of which I may take two works equally admirable in their respective lines. Mr. Austin,[53] in his *Lectures on Jurisprudence,* takes for his basis the Roman law, the most elaborately consistent legal system which history has shown us in actual operation and that which the greatest number of accomplished minds have employed themselves in harmonising. From this he singles out the principles and distinctions which are of general applicability, and employs the powers and resources of a most precise and analytic mind to give to those principles and distinctions a philosophic basis grounded in the universal reason of mankind and not in mere technical convenience. Mr. Maine, in his treatise on *Ancient Law in its Relations to Modern Thought,*[54] shows from the history of law and from what is known of the primitive institutions of mankind the origin of much that has lasted till now and has a firm footing both in the laws and in the ideas of modern times; showing that many of these things never originated in reason, but are relics of the institutions of barbarous society, modified more or less by civilisation, but kept standing by the persistency of ideas which were the offspring of those barbarous institutions and have survived their parent. The path opened up by

---

tion to the Principles of Morals and Legislation (1789) and *Rationale of Judicial Evidence* (1827) were valuable additions to legal theory. See above, p. 46 and note.—F. W. G.

[53] See above, pp. 93–94 and note.—F. W. G.

[54] Sir Harry Maine, a famous jurist; his *Ancient Law* was published in 1861.—F. W. G.

Mr. Maine has been followed up by others, with additional illustrations of the influence of obsolete ideas on modern institutions and of obsolete institutions on modern ideas—an action and reaction which perpetuate in many of the greatest concerns a mitigated barbarism, things being continually accepted as dictates of nature and necessities of life which, if we knew all, we should see to have originated in artificial arrangements of society long since abandoned and condemned.

To these studies I would add international law, which I decidedly think should be taught in all universities and should form part of all liberal education. The need of it is far from being limited to diplomatists and lawyers; it extends to every citizen. What is called the Law of Nations is not properly law, but a part of ethics, a set of moral rules accepted as authoritative by civilised states. It is true that these rules neither are nor ought to be of eternal obligation, but do and must vary more or less from age to age, as the consciences of nations become more enlightened and the exigences of political society undergo change. But the rules mostly were at their origin, and still are, an application of the maxims of honesty and humanity to the intercourse of states. They were introduced by the moral sentiments of mankind, or by their sense of the general interest, to mitigate the crimes and sufferings of a state of war and to restrain governments and nations from unjust or dishonest conduct towards one another in time of peace. Since every country stands in numerous and various relations with the other countries of the world and many, our own among the number, exercise actual authority over some of these, a knowledge of the established rules of international morality is essential to the duty of every nation and therefore of every person in it who helps to make up the nation and whose voice and feeling form a part of what is called public opinion. Let not anyone pacify his conscience by the delusion that he can do no harm if he takes no part and forms no opinion. Bad men need nothing more to compass their ends than that good men should look on and do nothing. He is not a good man who, without a protest, allows wrong to be committed in his name and with the means which he helps to supply, because he will not trouble himself to use his mind on the subject. It depends on the habit of attending to and looking into public transactions, and on the degree of information and solid judgement respecting them that exists in the community, whether the conduct of the nation as a nation, both within itself and towards others, shall be selfish, corrupt and tyrannical or rational and enlightened, just and noble.

Of these more advanced studies only a small commencement can be made at schools and universities; but even this is of the highest value by awakening an interest in the subjects, by conquering the first difficulties and inuring the mind to the kind of exertion which the studies require, by implanting a desire to make further progress and directing the student to the best tracks and the best helps. So far as these branches of knowledge have been acquired, we have learnt, or been put in the way of learning, our duty and our work in life. Knowing it, however, is but half the work of education; it still remains that what we know we shall be willing and determined to put into practice. Nevertheless, to know the truth is already a great way towards disposing us to act upon it. What we see clearly and apprehend keenly we have a natural desire to act out. "To see the best and yet the worst pursue," is a possible but not a common state of mind; those who follow the wrong have generally first taken care to be voluntarily ignorant of the right. They have silenced their conscience, but they are not knowingly disobeying it. If you take an average human mind while still young, before the objects it has chosen in life have given it a turn in any bad direction, you will generally find it desiring what is good, right and for the benefit of all; and if that season is properly used to implant the knowledge and give the training which shall render rectitude of judgement more habitual than sophistry, a serious barrier will have been erected against the inroads of selfishness and falsehood.[55] Still, it is a very imperfect education which trains the intelligence only but not the will. No one can dispense with an education directed expressly to the moral as well as the intellectual part of his being. Such education, so far as it is direct, is either moral or religious; and these may either be treated as distinct or as different aspects of the same thing. The subject we are now considering is not education as a whole, but scholastic education, and we must keep in view the inevitable limitations of what schools and universities can do. It is beyond their power to educate morally or religiously. Moral and religious education consist in training the feelings and the daily habits; and these are, in the main, beyond the sphere and inaccessible to the control of public education. It is the home, the family, which gives us the moral or religious education we really receive; and this is completed and modified, sometimes for the better, often for the worse, by society and the opinions and feelings with which we are there surrounded.[56] The moral or religious influence

[55] There are echoes here of Plato's *Republic* and Rousseau's *Emile*.—F. W. G.

[56] Mill rightly emphasizes the moral influence of home and society, but to say that "it is beyond the power" of schools to edu-

which a university can exercise consists less in any express teaching than in the pervading tone of the place. Whatever it teaches, it should teach as penetrated by a sense of duty; it should present all knowledge as chiefly a means to worthiness of life, given for the double purpose of making each of us practically useful to his fellow-creatures and of elevating the character of the species itself, exalting and dignifying our nature. There is nothing which spreads more contagiously from teacher to pupil than elevation of sentiment; often and often have students caught from the living influence of a professor a contempt for mean and selfish objects and a noble ambition to leave the world better than they found it, which they have carried with them throughout life. In these respects teachers of every kind have natural and peculiar means of doing with effect what everyone who mixes with his fellow-beings or addresses himself to them in any character should feel bound to do to the extent of his capacity and opportunities. What is special to a university on these subjects belongs chiefly, like the rest of its work, to the intellectual department. A university exists for the purpose of laying open to each succeeding generation, as far as the conditions of the case admit, the accumulated treasure of the thoughts of mankind. As an indispensable part of this it has to make known to them what mankind at large, their own country and the best and wisest individual men have thought on the great subjects of morals and religion. There should be, and there is in most universities, professorial instruction in moral philosophy; but I could wish that this instruction were of a somewhat different type from what is ordinar-

---

cate morally is surely incorrect; what he says about the "pervading tone" of a university applies with equal, perhaps greater, force to schools.—F. W. G.

ily met with. I could wish that it were more expository, less polemical and above all less dogmatic. The learner should be made acquainted with the principal systems of moral philosophy which have existed and been practically operative among mankind, and should hear what there is to be said for each: the Aristotelian, the Epicurean, the Stoic, the Judaic, the Christian in the various modes of its interpretation, which differ almost as much from one another as the teachings of those earlier schools. He should be made familiar with the different standards of right and wrong which have been taken as the basis of ethics: general utility, natural justice, natural rights, a moral sense, principles of practical reason and the rest. Among all these it is not so much the teacher's business to take a side and fight stoutly for some one against the rest, as it is to direct them all towards the establishment and preservation of the rules of conduct most advantageous to mankind. There is not one of these systems which has not its good side; not one from which there is not something to be learnt by the votaries of the others; not one which is not suggested by a keen, though it may not always be a clear, perception of some important truths, which are the prop of the system and the neglect or undervaluing of which in other systems is their characteristic infirmity. A system which may be as a whole erroneous is still valuable until it has forced upon mankind a sufficient attention to the portion of truth which suggested it. The ethical teacher does his part best when he points out how each system may be strengthened, even on its own basis, by taking into more complete account the truths which other systems have realised more fully and made more prominent. I do not mean that he should encourage an essentially sceptical eclecticism. While placing every system in the best aspect it admits of and endeavouring to draw from all of them the most salutary consequences compatible with their nature, I would by no means debar him from enforcing by his best arguments his own preference for some one of the number. They cannot be all true, though those which are false as theories may contain particular truths indispensable to the completeness of the true theory. But on this subject, even more than on any of those I have previously mentioned, it is not the teacher's business to impose his own judgement, but to inform and discipline that of his pupil.

And this same clue, if we keep hold of it, will guide us through the labyrinth of conflicting thought into which we enter when we touch the great question of the relation of education to religion.[57] As I have already said, the only really effective religious education is the parental—that of home and childhood. All that social and public education has in its power to do, further than by a general pervading tone of reverence and duty, amounts to little more than the information which it can give; but this is extremely valuable. I shall not enter into the question which has been debated with so much vehemence in the last and present generation whether religion ought to be taught at all in universities and public schools, seeing that religion is the subject of all others on which men's opinions are most widely at variance. On neither side of this controversy do the disputants seem to me to have sufficiently freed their minds from the old notion of education that it consists in the dogmatic inculcation from authority of what the teacher deems true. Why should it be impossible that informa-

[57] In the following comments on religious education there is much of relevance to current discussion both in Britain and the U.S.A.—F. W. G.

tion of the greatest value on subjects connected with religion should be brought before the student's mind; that he should be made acquainted with so important a part of the national thought and of the intellectual labours of past generations as those relating to religion, without being taught dogmatically the doctrines of any church or sect? Christianity being a historical religion, the sort of religious instruction which seems to me most appropriate to a university is the study of ecclesiastical history. If teaching, even on matters of scientific certainty, should aim quite as much at showing how the results are arrived at as at teaching the results themselves, far more, then, should this be the case on subjects where there is the widest diversity of opinion among men of equal ability and who have taken equal pains to arrive at the truth. This diversity should of itself be a warning to a conscientious teacher that he has no right to impose his opinion authoritatively upon a youthful mind. His teaching should not be in the spirit of dogmatism, but in that of enquiry. The pupil should not be addressed as if his religion had been chosen for him, but as one who will have to choose it for himself. The various Churches, established and unestablished, are quite competent to the task which is peculiarly theirs, that of teaching each its own doctrines, as far as necessary, to its own rising generation. The proper business of a university is different: not to tell us from authority what we ought to believe and make us accept the belief as a duty, but to give us information and training, and help us to form our own belief in a manner worthy of intelligent beings who seek for truth at all hazards and demand to know all the difficulties, in order that they may be better qualified to find, or recognise, the most satisfactory mode of resolving them. The vast importance of these questions—the great results, as regards the conduct of our lives, which depend upon our choosing one belief or another—are the strongest reasons why we should not trust our judgement when it has been formed in ignorance of the evidence, and why we should not consent to be restricted to a one-sided teaching which informs us of what a particular teacher or association of teachers receive as true doctrine and sound argument, but of nothing more.

I do not affirm that a university, if it represses free thought and enquiry, must be altogether a failure, for the freest thinkers have often been trained in the most slavish seminaries of learning. The great Christian reformers were taught in Roman Catholic universities; the sceptical philosophers of France were mostly educated by the Jesuits.[58] The human mind is sometimes impelled all the more violently in one direction by an over zealous and demonstrative attempt to drag it in the opposite. But this is not what universities are appointed for—to drive men from them, even into good, by excess of evil. A university ought to be a place of free speculation.[59] The more diligently it does its duty in all other respects, the more certain it is to be that. The old English universities in the present generation are doing better work than they have done within human memory in teaching the ordinary studies of their curriculum; and one of the consequences has been that, whereas they formerly seemed to exist mainly for the repression of independent thought and the chaining up of the individual intellect and conscience, they are now the great foci of free and manly enquiry to the higher and professional

[58] For instance, Luther and Descartes respectively.—F. W. G.

[59] On the reception accorded to this passage of the *Address* see above, p. 27.—F. W. G.

classes south of the Tweed.[60] The ruling minds of those ancient seminaries have at last remembered that to place themselves in hostility to the free use of the understanding is to abdicate their own best privilege, that of guiding it. A modest deference, at least provisional, to the united authority of the specially instructed is becoming in a youthful and imperfectly formed mind; but when there is no united authority—when the specially instructed are so divided and scattered that almost any opinion can boast of some high authority and no opinion whatever can claim all; when, therefore, it can never be deemed extremely improbable that one who uses his mind freely may see reason to change his first opinion; then, whatever you do, keep at all risks your minds open; do not barter away your freedom of thought. Those of you who are destined for the clerical profession are, no doubt, so far held to a certain number of doctrines that, if they ceased to believe them, they would not be justified in remaining in a position in which they would be required to teach insincerely. But use your influence to make those doctrines as few as possible. It is not right that men should be bribed to hold out against conviction, to shut their ears against objections or, if the objections penetrate, to continue professing full and unfaltering belief when their confidence is already shaken. Neither is it right that, if men honestly profess to have changed some of their religious opinions, their honesty should as a matter of course exclude them from taking a part for which they may be admirably qualified in the spiritual instruction of the nation. The tendency of the age on both sides of the ancient Border

[60] The border between England and Scotland.—F. W. G.

is towards the relaxation of formularies and a less rigid construction of articles. This very circumstance, by making the limits of orthodoxy less definite and obliging everyone to draw the line for himself, is an embarrassment to consciences. But I hold entirely with those clergymen who elect to remain in the national church, so long as they are able to accept its articles and confessions in any sense or with any interpretation consistent with common honesty, whether it be the generally received interpretation or not. If all were to desert the church who put a large and liberal construction on its terms of communion or who would wish to see those terms widened, the national provision for religious teaching and worship would be left utterly to those who take the narrowest, the most literal and purely textual view of the formularies; who, though by no means necessarily bigots, are under the great disadvantage of having the bigots for their allies, and who, however great their merits may be—and they are often very great—yet if the church is improvable, are not the most likely persons to improve it. Therefore, if it were not an impertinence in me to tender advice in such a matter, I should say, let all who conscientiously can remain in the church. A church is far more easily improved from within than from without. Almost all the illustrious reformers of religion began by being clergymen; but they did not think that their profession as clergymen was inconsistent with being reformers. They mostly indeed ended their days outside the churches in which they were born; but it was because the churches, in an evil hour for themselves, cast them out. They did not think it any business of theirs to withdraw. They thought they had a better right to remain in the fold than those had who expelled them.

I have now said what I had to say on the two kinds of education which the system of schools and universities is intended to promote, intellectual education and moral education—knowledge and the training of the knowing faculty, conscience and that of the moral faculty. These are the two main ingredients of human culture; but they do not exhaust the whole of it. There is a third division which, if subordinate and owing allegiance to the two others, is barely inferior to them and not less needful to the completeness of the human being; I mean the aesthetic branch, the culture which comes through poetry and art and may be described as the education of the feelings and the cultivation of the beautiful. This department of things deserves to be regarded in a far more serious light than is the custom of these countries. It is only of late, and chiefly by a superficial imitation of foreigners, that we have begun to use the word Art by itself and to speak of Art as we speak of Science or Government or Religion; we used to talk of the Arts, and more specifically of the Fine Arts—and even by them were vulgarly meant only two forms of art, painting and sculpture, the two which as a people we cared least about, which were regarded even by the more cultivated among us as little more than branches of domestic ornamentation, a kind of elegant upholstery. The very words "Fine Arts" called up a notion of frivolity, of great pains expended on a rather trifling object—on something which differed from the cheaper and commoner arts of producing pretty things mainly by being more difficult and by giving fops an opportunity of pluming themselves on caring for it and on being able to talk about it. This estimate extended in no small degree, though not altogether, even to poetry, the queen of arts, but in Great

Britain hardly included under the name.[61] It cannot exactly be said that poetry was little thought of; we were proud of our Shakespeare and Milton, and in one period at least of our history, that of Queen Anne, it was a high literary distinction to be a poet; but poetry was hardly looked upon in any serious light or as having much value except as an amusement or excitement, the superiority of which over others principally consisted in being that of a more refined order of minds. Yet the celebrated saying of Fletcher of Saltoun,[62] "Let who will make the laws of a people if I write their songs," might have taught us how great an instrument for acting on the human mind we were undervaluing. It would be difficult for anybody to imagine that "Rule Britannia,"[63] for example, or "Scots wha hae,"[64] had no permanent influence on the higher region of human character; some of Moore's songs have done more for Ireland than all Grattan's

[61] For instance, John Locke, in *Thoughts concerning Education* (1693), writes: "It [music] wastes so much of a young man's time to gain but a moderate skill in it, and engages often in such odd company that many think it much better spared" (§ 197); and: "If he [the child] have a poetic vein, 'tis to me the strangest thing in the world that the father should desire or suffer it to be cherished or improved" (§ 174).—F. W. G.

[62] Andrew Fletcher (1655–1716), a Scottish patriot. The quotation comes from *An Account of a Conversation concerning a Right Regulation of Governments for the Common Good of Mankind* (1704): "I knew a very wise man so much of Sir Christopher [Musgrave's] sentiment that he believed if a man were permitted to make all the ballads, he need not care who should make the laws of a nation"—an echo, possibly, of Plato; see The *Republic,* ed. H. D. P. Lee (Harmondsworth: Penguin Books, 1955), pp. 169-170.—F. W. G.

[63] Written by James Thomson; see above, p. 148.—F. W. G.

[64] From the poem of Robert Burns:

> "Scots, wha hae [who have] wi' Wallace bled,
> Scots, wham Bruce has aften led. . . ."

—F. W. G.

speeches;[65] and songs are far from being the highest or most impressive form of poetry. On these subjects the mode of thinking and feeling of other countries was not only not intelligible, but not credible, to an average Englishman. To find Art ranking on a complete equality, in theory at least, with Philosophy, Learning and Science—as holding an equally important place among the agents of civilisation and among the elements of the worth of humanity; to find even painting and sculpture treated as great social powers, and the art of a country as a feature in its character and condition little inferior in importance to either its religion or its government—all this only did not amaze and puzzle Englishmen because it was too strange for them to be able to realise it or, in truth, to believe it possible; and the radical difference of feeling on this matter between the British people and those of France, Germany and the Continent generally is one among the causes of that extraordinary inability to understand one another which exists between England and the rest of Europe, while it does not exist to anything like the same degree between one nation of continental Europe and another. It may be traced to the two influences which have chiefly shaped the British character since the days of the Stuarts, commercial money-getting business, and religious Puritanism: business, demanding the whole of the faculties and, whether pursued from duty or the love of gain, regarding as a loss of time whatever does not conduce directly to the end; Puritanism, which, looking upon every feeling of human

[65] Thomas Moore (1779–1852), Irish poet and writer of songs; his *Irish Melodies,* in which he wrote the words for existing tunes, was immensely popular. Henry Grattan (1748–1820), an Irish politician devoted to the cause of Irish independence, and an orator of great eloquence.—F. W. G.

nature except fear and reverence for God as a snare, if not as partaking of sin, looked coldly, if not disapprovingly, on the cultivation of the sentiments. Different causes have produced different effects in the continental nations, among whom it is even now observable that virtue and goodness are generally for the most part an affair of the sentiments, while with us they are almost exclusively an affair of duty. Accordingly, the kind of advantage which we have had over many other countries in point of morals—I am not sure that we are not losing it—has consisted in greater tenderness of conscience. In this we have had on the whole a real superiority, though one principally negative; for conscience is with most men a power chiefly in the way of restraint, a power which acts rather in staying our hands from any great wickedness than by the direction it gives to the general course of our desires and sentiments. One of the commonest types of character among us is that of a man all whose ambition is self-regarding; who has no higher purpose in life than to enrich or raise in the world himself and his family; who never dreams of making the good of his fellow-creatures or of his country an habitual object, further than giving away annually or from time to time certain sums in charity; but who has a conscience sincerely alive to whatever is generally considered wrong, and would scruple to use any very illegitimate means for attaining his self-interested objects. While it will often happen in other countries that men whose feelings and whose active energies point strongly in an unselfish direction, who have the love of their country, of human improvement, of human freedom, even of virtue, in great strength, and of whose thoughts and activity a large share is devoted to disinterested objects, will yet in the pursuit of these or of any other objects that they strongly desire permit themselves to do wrong things which the other man, though intrinsically and taking the whole of his character farther removed from what a human being ought to be, could not bring himself to commit. It is of no use to debate which of these two states of mind is the best, or rather the least bad. It is quite possible to cultivate the conscience and the sentiments too. Nothing hinders us from so training a man that he will not, even for a disinterested purpose, violate the moral law, and also feeding and encouraging those high feelings on which we mainly rely for lifting men above low and sordid objects and giving them a higher conception of what constitutes success in life. If we wish men to practise virtue, it is worth while trying to make them love virtue and feel it an object in itself and not a tax paid for leave to pursue other objects. It is worth training them to feel not only actual wrong or actual meanness, but the absence of noble aims and endeavours as not merely blamable but also degrading; to have a feeling of the miserable smallness of mere self in the face of this great universe, of the collective mass of our fellow creatures, in the face of past history and of the indefinite future—the poorness and insignificance of human life if it is to be all spent in making things comfortable for ourselves and our kin and raising ourselves and them a step or two on the social ladder. Thus feeling, we learn to respect ourselves only so far as we feel capable of nobler objects; and if, unfortunately, those by whom we are surrounded do not share our aspirations, perhaps disapprove the conduct to which we are prompted by them, [we learn] to sustain ourselves by the ideal sympathy of the great characters in history or even in fiction, and by the contemplation of an idealised posterity—shall I add, of ideal perfection embodied in a Divine Being? Now, of this elevated tone of mind the great source of inspiration is poetry, and all literature so far as it is poetical and artistic. We may imbibe exalted feelings from Plato or Demosthenes or Tacitus, but it is so far as those great men are not solely philosophers or orators or historians, but poets and artists. Nor is it only loftiness, only the heroic feelings, that are bred by poetic cultivation. Its power is as great in calming the soul as in elevating it—in fostering the milder emotions, as the more exalted. It brings home to us all those aspects of life which take hold of our nature on its unselfish side and lead us to identify our joy and grief with the good or ill of the system of which we form a part; and all those solemn or pensive feelings which, without having any direct application to conduct, incline us to take life seriously and predispose us to the reception of anything which comes before us in the shape of duty. Who does not feel himself a better man after a course of Dante or of Wordsworth or, I will add, of Lucretius or the *Georgics*,[66] or after brooding over Gray's *Elegy* or Shelley's *Hymn to Intellectual Beauty*? I have spoken of poetry, but all the other modes of art produce similar effects in their degree. The races and nations whose senses are naturally finer and their sensuous perceptions more exercised than ours receive the same kind of impressions from painting and sculpture; and many of the more delicately organised among ourselves do the same. All the arts of expression tend to keep alive and in activity the feelings they express. Do you think that the great Italian painters would have filled the place they did in the European mind, would have been universally ranked among the greatest men of their time, if their productions had done nothing

[66] On Lucretius see above, p. 138; the *Georgics* was a poem of Virgil on farming and country life.—F. W. G.

for it but to serve as the decoration of a public hall or a private *salon?* Their Nativities and Crucifixions, their glorious Madonnas and Saints, were to their susceptible southern countrymen the great school not only of the devotional, but of all the elevated and all the imaginative feelings. We colder northerns may approach to a conception of this function of art when we listen to an oratorio of Handel or give ourselves up to the emotions excited by a Gothic cathedral. Even apart from any specific emotional expression, the mere contemplation of beauty of a high order produces in no small degree this elevating effect on the character. The power of natural scenery addresses itself to the same region of human nature which corresponds to Art.[67] There are few capable of feeling the sublimer order of natural beauty, such as your own Highlands and other mountain regions afford, who are not, at least temporarily, raised by it above the littlenesses of humanity and made to feel the puerility of the petty objects which set men's interests at variance contrasted with the nobler pleasures which all might share. To whatever avocations we may be called in life, let us never quash those susceptibilities within us, but carefully seek the opportunities of maintaining them in exercise. The more prosaic our ordinary duties, the more necessary it is to keep up the tone of our minds by frequent visits to that higher region of thought and feeling in which every work seems dignified in proportion to the ends for which and the spirit in which it is done; where we learn, while eagerly seizing every opportunity of

[67] It is clear from Mill's *Autobiography* and from his letters, as well as from his leisure pursuits of walking and botanizing, that he had a great love of the countryside and natural scenery; for example, see above, pp. 86, 87, 131, and Bain's *John Stuart Mill,* pp. 151-154.—F. W. G.

exercising higher faculties and performing higher duties, to regard all useful and honest work as a public function, which may be ennobled by the mode of performing it—which has not properly any other nobility than what that gives—and which, if ever so humble, is never mean but when it is meanly done and when the motives from which it is done are mean motives. There is, besides, a natural affinity between goodness and the cultivation of the Beautiful, when it is real cultivation and not a mere unguided instinct. He who has learnt what beauty is, if he be of a virtuous character, will desire to realise it in his own life, will keep before himself a type of perfect beauty in human character to light his attempts at self-culture. There is a true meaning in the saying of Goethe,[68] though liable to be misunderstood and perverted, that the Beautiful is greater than the Good; for it includes the Good and adds something to it; it is the Good made perfect and fitted with all the collateral perfections which make it a finished and completed thing. Now this sense of perfection, which would make us demand from every creation of man the very utmost that it ought to give and render us intolerant of the smallest fault in ourselves or in anything we do, is one of the results of Art cultivation. No other human productions come so near to perfection as works of pure Art. In all other things we are, and may reasonably be, satisfied if the degree of excellence is as great as the object immediately in view seems to us to be worth; but in Art the perfection is itself the object. If I were to define Art, I should be inclined to call it the endeavour after perfection in execution. If we meet with even a piece of mechanical work which bears the marks of being done in

[68] I cannot trace this reference.—F. W. G.

this spirit—which is done as if the workman loved it and tried to make it as good as possible, though something less good would have answered the purpose for which it was ostensibly made—we say that he has worked like an artist. Art, when really cultivated and not merely practised empirically, maintains what it first gave the conception of, an ideal Beauty to be eternally aimed at, though surpassing what can be actually attained; and by this idea it trains us never to be completely satisfied with imperfection in what we ourselves do and are, to idealise as much as possible every work we do and most of all our own characters and lives.

And now, having travelled with you over the whole range of the materials and training which a university supplies as a preparation for the higher uses of life, it is almost needless to add any exhortation to you to profit by the gift. Now is your opportunity for gaining a degree of insight into subjects larger and far more ennobling than the minutiae of a business or a profession, and for acquiring a facility of using your minds on all that concerns the higher interests of man which you will carry with you into the occupations of active life and which will prevent even the short intervals of time which that may leave you from being altogether lost for noble purposes. Having once conquered the first difficulties—the only ones of which the irksomeness surpasses the interest—having turned the point beyond which what was once a task becomes a pleasure, in even the busiest after-life the higher powers of your mind will make progress imperceptibly by the spontaneous exercise of your thoughts and by the lessons you will know how to learn from daily experience. So, at least, it will be, if in your early studies you have fixed your eyes upon the ultimate end from which those studies take their chief value—that of making you more effective combatants in the great fight which never ceases to rage between Good and Evil, and more equal to coping with the ever new problems which the changing course of human nature and human society present to be resolved. Aims like these commonly retain the footing which they have once established in the mind; and their presence in our thoughts keeps our higher faculties in exercise and makes us consider the acquirements and powers which we store up at any time of our lives as a mental capital to be freely expended in helping forward any mode which presents itself of making mankind in any respect wiser or better, or placing any portion of human affairs on a more sensible and rational footing than its existing one. There is not one of us who may not qualify himself so to improve the average amount of opportunities as to leave his fellow creatures some little the better for the use he has known how to make of his intellect. To make this little greater, let us strive to keep ourselves acquainted with the best thoughts that are brought forth by the original minds of the age, that we may know what movements stand most in need of our aid, and that, as far as depends on us, the good seed may not fall on a rock and perish without reaching the soil in which it might have germinated and flourished. You are to be a part of the public who are to welcome, encourage and help forward the future intellectual benefactors of humanity; and you are, if possible, to furnish your contingent to the number of those benefactors. Nor let anyone be discouraged by what may seem, in moments of despondency, the lack of time and of opportunity. Those who know how to employ opportunities will often find that they can create them; and what we achieve depends less on the amount of time we possess than on the use we make of our time.

You and your like are the hope and resource of your country in the coming generation. All great things which that generation is destined to do have to be done by some like you; several will assuredly be done by persons for whom society has done much less, to whom it has given far less preparation than those whom I am now addressing. I do not attempt to instigate you by the prospect of direct rewards, either earthly or heavenly; the less we think about being rewarded in either way, the better for us. But there is one reward which will not fail you and which may be called disinterested because it is not a consequence, but is inherent in the very fact of deserving it—the deeper and more varied interest you will feel in life, which will give it tenfold its value, and a value which will last to the end. All merely personal objects grow less valuable as we advance in life: this not only endures but increases.

Index

FRANCIS W. GARFORTH, Lecturer in Education at the University of Hull, England, was born in Ceylon in 1917. He received his B.A. from the University of London and his M.A. from Cambridge University. After teaching in secondary schools for ten years, he joined the university's Department of Education in 1949. Mr. Garforth is the author of *Education and Social Purpose* (1962) and *The Scope of Philosophy* (1971). He has edited the volumes *Locke's Thoughts Concerning Education* (1964), *John Dewey: Selected Educational Writings* (1966), and a selection from Bede's *Historia Ecclesiastica* (1967); he has also contributed *John Locke's "Of the Conduct of the Understanding"* (1966) to the Classics in Education series.